WITH PURPOSE AND PRINCIPLE

With Purpose and Principle

Essays About the Seven Principles
of Unitarian Universalism

EDITED BY EDWARD A. FROST

Skinner House Books
Boston

ISBN 1-55896-369-3

Printed in the USA.

10 9 8 7 6 5 4 3 2 1
02 01 00 99 98

PRINCIPLES AND PURPOSES

We, the member congregations of the Unitarian Universalist Association, covenant to affirm and promote:

- The inherent worth and dignity of every person
- Justice, equity, and compassion in human relations
- Acceptance of one another and encouragement to spiritual growth in our congregations
- A free and responsible search for truth and meaning
- The right of conscience and the use of the democratic process within our congregations and in society at large
- The goal of world community with peace, liberty, and justice for all
- Respect for the interdependent web of all existence of which we are a part.

The living tradition we share draws from many sources:

- Direct experience of that transcending mystery and wonder, affirmed in all cultures, which moves us to a renewal of the spirit and an openness to the forces which create and uphold life
- Words and deeds of prophetic women and men which challenge us to confront powers and structures of evil with justice, compassion, and the transforming power of love

- Wisdom from the world's religions which inspires us in our ethical and spiritual life
- Jewish and Christian teaching which call us to respond to God's love by loving our neighbors as ourselves
- Humanist teachings which counsel us to heed the guidance of reason and the results of science, and warn us against idolatries of the mind and spirit
- Spiritual teachings of Earth-centered traditions which celebrate the sacred circle of life and instruct us to live in harmony with the rhythms of nature.

The Unitarian Universalist Association shall devote its resources to and exercise its corporate powers for religious, educational, and humanitarian purposes. The primary purpose of the Association is to serve the needs of its member congregations, organize new congregations, extend and strengthen Unitarian Universalist institutions, and implement its principles.

CONTENTS

Preface   ix

Introduction   1

From Grailville to Atlanta: 9
A Delicate and Dangerous Path

We Affirm and Promote   23
    The Inherent Worth and Dignity
    of Every Person
        Marilyn Sewell

We Affirm and Promote   31
    Justice, Equity, and Compassion
    in Human Relations
        Richard S. Gilbert

We Affirm and Promote   45
    Acceptance of One Another and
    Encouragement to Spiritual Growth
    in Our Congregations
        Carolyn Owen-Towle

We Affirm and Promote   53
    A Free and Responsible Search for
    Truth and Meaning
        Fredric Muir

We Affirm and Promote   69
 The Right of Conscience and the
 Use of the Democratic Process Within
 Our Congregations and in Society at Large
  Earl K. Holt III

We Affirm and Promote   79
 The Goal of World Community With
 Peace, Liberty, and Justice for All
  John Buehrens

We Affirm and Promote   91
 Respect for the Interdependent Web of
 All Existence of Which We Are a Part
  Barbara Merritt

Common Beliefs   103

Appendix A: Bylaws of the Unitarian Universalist   109
 Association, 1961-1984

Appendix B: The Women and Religion Resolution   111

Appendix C: 1981 Proposed Bylaw Amendment   113

Appendix D: New Draft Amendment   115

Further Reading   117

PREFACE

My thanks to my colleagues for their contribution to this work. Marilyn Sewell, Minister of First Unitarian Church of Portland, Oregon; Richard Gilbert, Minister of the First Unitarian Church of Rochester, New York; Carolyn Owen-Towle, Co-Minister of the First Unitarian Church of San Diego, California; Fredric Muir, Minister of the Unitarian Universalist Church of Annapolis, Maryland; Earl Holt III, Minister of the First Unitarian Church of St. Louis, Missouri; John Buehrens, President of the Unitarian Universalist Association; and Barbara Merritt, Minister of the First Unitarian Church of Worcester, Massachusetts.

I also wish to thank Ms. Elinor Artman and Ms. Lucile Schuck Longview for their reading of my chapter on the history of the Purposes and Principles and for their suggestions and recommendations.

Walter Royal Jones, a Unitarian Universalist minister, now retired, was generous with his time and packets of materials, willing, once again, to tell the story of the UUA Principles and Purposes. Unitarian Universalists are indebted to the Reverend Jones for his leadership of the Committee to Revise the Purposes and Principles.

Article II of the bylaws of the Unitarian Universalist Association, the subject of this book, has three distinctive segments: the principles of the Association (see the first seven statements on page v), the purposes of the Association (see the last paragraph on page vi), and the sources (see the second six statements on pages v-vi), referred to as "the living tradition," from which Unitarian Universalists draw sustenance for their diverse faith. The reader will note that, though reference is continually made in this work to the UUA Principles and Purposes, little is said about the purposes and scant attention is paid to the sources section of the bylaws. As to the purposes, I have written little simply because, in my opinion, they are self-explanatory. They deal with the practical mission of the Unitarian Universalist Association, and, in the final words of the statement, it is stated that a primary purpose of the Association is to implement its principles. The sources, while certainly the cause of considerable debate and struggle, would require at least one book of their own. The focus of this book, therefore, is on the principles: how they came to be and what they mean to Unitarian Universalists.

Edward A. Frost

Introduction

It is often said that Unitarian Universalists have no creed. The Reverend Paul Carnes, former president of the Unitarian Universalist Association, once stated that within Unitarian Universalism is "a fear of creedalism that is irrational to the point of being dogmatic" (*The Free Church in a Changing World*). When asked what Unitarian Universalism is, a common—and unfortunate—response is something like, "We can believe whatever we want to believe." A television host, who had picked up a popular definition of Unitarian Universalism somewhere, once defined my faith for me, on camera, as one whose adherents "believe a little bit of what all the other religions believe." Before I could prevent it, that impression of a religious smorgasbord was stamped on the Public Broadcasting System audience, and the microphone and the camera moved on.

Without question, the emphasis in Unitarian Universalism is on diversity, individual freedom of belief, and the autonomy of the local congregation. But can a religious association without a common faith have any significant claim on its members, let alone any significant influence in the world? Philosopher of religion Henry Nelson Wieman, although sympathetic to Unitarianism, stated unequivocally that it could not. Without a common faith, Wieman insisted, there can be no "power of assembly." Without a common faith, he said, congregations are likely to be little more than "talking clubs of individualists."

Fear of creeds notwithstanding, our Unitarian and Universalist forebears knew well enough that a religion needs to be able to say to the world what it is that its adherents believe. The difficulty, for these free churches, lay in formulating what could be said without usurping the freedom of belief cherished and firmly defended by their members. They struggled from the beginning to express their beliefs in statements that might create the strength of unity while preserving the freedom and diversity each movement held precious. The principles and purposes statement, incorporated into the bylaws of the Unitarian Universalist Association, is but the latest in a long history of attempts to state, if not a common faith, at least a workable consensus about what brings us together.

In 1803, at a convention in Winchester, New Hampshire, the Universalists adopted the Winchester Confession, a statement of belief that affirmed the central doctrine of the new American religion, that in God's love and forbearance, all souls will be saved. The reigning Calvinist doctrine of election proclaimed that some would be saved and some damned, according to God's inscrutable will, regardless of what they did or did not do. The Winchester Confession stated that God "will finally restore the whole family of mankind to holiness and happiness." A "liberty clause" was included in the Confession under which local congregations could adopt their own statements of faith and belief "provided they do not disagree with our general profession. . . ."

Was the Winchester Confession a creed? That depends on how we define creed. Of the many definitions, two will be enough for our purposes. One interpretation was suggested by historian Philip Schaff: "A creed, or rule of Faith, or Symbol, is a confession of faith for public use, or a form of words setting forth with authority certain articles of belief, which are regarded by the framers as being necessary for salvation, or at least for the well-being of the Christian Church" (*History of the Creeds of Christendom*).

Unitarian Universalist historian Robert Hemstreet offers a narrower definition. A creed, he writes, is a "definitive statement of a church doctrine to which one must subscribe to be a full member of a particular church" (*Identity and Ideology*). Because, in spite of the "liberty clause," the Winchester Confession did not permit local statements to disagree with the general confession, it seems that, at least in Schaff's broader sense, it was indeed a creed. Many Universalists objected strenuously to the statement, insisting on the right to personal interpretation. But the denomination held fast, even dropping the "liberty clause" in 1877.

In 1899 and again in 1935, the Universalists adopted new professions of faith framed in more contemporary language. The new professions also affirmed that "no precise form of words" would be required of ministers or members. The Universalist Church, from its earliest beginnings, proclaimed—and documented—its common faith of universal salvation.

The Universalists had developed professions, confessions, or creeds that could be recited in Sunday services and taught in Sunday schools. The statements also clearly defined the new sect among American religions. If one wanted to know what Universalists believed, one could simply turn to the Winchester Confession or to the later statements that evolved from it. The Boston Profession of 1899, for example, lent itself handily to many series of sermons on the meaning of Universalism.

Unitarian history is not so straightforward. Unlike Universalism, Unitarianism in America did not begin as a new sect to be publicly, plainly defined. Unitarianism—essentially grounded in the rejection of the doctrine of the Trinity and in the teachings and example of the human Jesus—was, in its earliest days, a movement within the congregations of the established churches of New England. Not all the members of those churches were Unitarians in their beliefs. No statement of Unitarian faith or principle would be read within their walls. The principles of the religious movement were expressed, therefore, not corporately, but by individuals, particularly by the ministers who preached the Unitarian message, and by religious associations.

One of those associations was the American Unitarian Association (AUA), founded in 1825 for the purpose of supporting missionaries and publishing religious tracts. During its first years, the AUA issued a statement expressing the predominantly practical emphasis of Unitarianism.

We value our doctrines only so far as they evidently are the revelation of the will and character of God and so far as they tend to improve the religious, moral, and intellectual condition of mankind. . . . The great end of this association is the promotion of pure morals and practical piety.

For its first one hundred years, the intent of the members of the Unitarian Association was to promote "pure Christianity" in the United States. "Pure Christianity" was understood as Christianity untainted by such dogma as the Trinity, the infallibility of scripture, and salvation through the atoning sacrifice of the God/man, Jesus. The bylaws of the Unitarian Association defined the Association primarily in practical terms and were not much concerned with doctrine.

Those one hundred years, however, were rife with theological struggle. Whatever unity in diversity had been enjoyed in the early years of that broadly inclusive statement of purpose began to unravel with the appearance on the religious scene of transcendentalism and, in the theological schools, the "Higher Criticism" of the Bible. Three prominent ministers added their eloquent voices to the struggle: Ralph Waldo Emerson preached his Divinity School Address, which not only the Boston ministers but also all of Harvard's Divinity School faculty declared appalling heresy. Theodore Parker's sermon at the ordination of Jared Sparks further defined Unitarianism beyond the pale even of "pure Christianity." William Ellery Channing, though he privately thought Parker had gone too far and was too "aggressive" in his tone, was himself called an "infidel" by many of his colleagues.

The struggle rocked back and forth between those who wished to keep the Unitarian Association solidly Christian, that is, grounded solely in the teaching and example of Jesus as known through the Christian scriptures, and those who would open its ranks to any who wanted to go beyond Christianity to "naturalistic" and ethically based religion (a quarrel that erupted again several generations later). Some attempts were made to establish creedal statements that would exclude those who strayed too far from Unitarian Christianity, but none were effective or lasting.

In 1894, after years of divisions and subdivisions related to virtually every matter of faith—the nature of God, of "man," the nature of Jesus, the fallibility or infallibility of scripture—a new preamble to the National Conference of Unitarian congregations (first gathered in 1865) was adopted. The key statement was, "These churches accept the religion of Jesus, holding in accordance with his teaching, that practical religion is summed up in love to God and love to man." The preamble continued to say that nothing in the constitution of the Conference was to be construed as an authoritative test and that all were welcome who were "in general sympathy with our spirit and our practical aims."

That all-embracing, thoroughly inoffensive statement ushered Unitarianism into a quarter-century period of untroubled theological slumber. The awakening came with the emergence, during the years of World War I, of openly nontheistic, humanist ministers, many of whom had been expelled from other denominations. In 1920, Curtis Reese gave a lecture at Harvard's Summer School of Theology outlining humanist views. His lecture led to a long humanist-theist debate in Unitarianism, culminating in the drafting of a resolution brought to the biennial National Conference in 1922 that would have excluded humanists from association. The proposal never came to the floor. Nevertheless, the strife between theistic and humanist Unitarians continued for the next thirty years.

During World War II, plans were laid for the expansion of Unitarianism, which had suffered serious depletion of membership in the years since the Great War. The American Unitarian Association's board set up committees on "Unitarian Advance." One of those committees, chaired by the revered minister A. Powell Davies, was charged with framing a statement that would set the theological ground for the growth of the movement. The committee drew up a list of five principles with which it believed most Unitarians would agree. The five principles were:

Individual freedom of belief; discipleship to advancing truth; the democratic process in human relations; universal brotherhood, undivided by nation, race, or creed; and allegiance to the cause of a united world community.

The principles were widely accepted, quoted in denominational literature, and included in the statements of purpose, covenants, and bonds of union of many congregations. When, in 1961, the American Unitarian Association merged with the Universalist Church, the five principles were incorporated into the new association's Statement of Purpose. Echoes of those principles can still be heard in the current Principles and Purposes of the Unitarian Universalist Association.

The Unitarian Universalist fear of creeds may well border on the irrational, as Paul Carnes suggested. Still, as this brief historical survey demonstrates, both movements have attempted continually through the years to formulate statements that would capture what it is that Unitarians and Universalists believe. Where these attempts have failed, they have failed for essentially two reasons: first, because most of the attempts to write a creed were intended or were interpreted as intending to exclude minority views and positions; and, secondly, because both Unitarians and Universalists have historically held fast to one unstated ideology—individualism. Any attempt to draw a circle might be interpreted as an attempt to shut some outside or as an attempt to keep some in. It is this embedded ideology of individualism that frustrated former attempts to proclaim a unity in theological diversity and that, as we shall see in the following chapter, made the road to a new statement of principle and purpose "delicate and dangerous."

—EAF

From Grailville to Atlanta: A Delicate and Dangerous Path

New occasions teach new duties.
Time makes ancient good uncouth.
—James Russell Lowell

By the late 1970s, the original statement of purposes and principles of the Unitarian Universalist Association (see Appendix A), forged in the merger conventions of the Universalist Church of America and the Unitarian Association in 1961 and incorporated into the new Association's bylaws, had become "uncouth." The statement had been drafted by men, mostly ministers. Gender word changes had been made later in the sixties and in 1976, but feminists believed that the goal of equality was far from being reached and that the UUA Principles and Purposes still reflected patriarchal and hierarchical assumptions. The term "brotherhood," for example, had survived the 1976 language revisions.

The theological language of the 1961 statement was also coming under increased criticism. To save the merger, there had been considerable compromise between traditional Christian and humanistic perspectives in Universalism and in Unitarianism. The principles referred to the teachers and prophets "in every age and tradition" but asserted that the truths they taught "are summarized in the Judeo-Christian heritage as love to God and love to humankind." In the 1970s, not everyone agreed, to say the least, that the great universal truths of the world's religions could be summed up in the Judeo-Christian tradition.

The 1970s were also an era of rising consciousness in the field of ecology. The original statement of principles did not reflect the growing sense of relatedness to the environment and our responsibility for it.

The path to change began in Lexington, Massachusetts, at First Parish, where Lucile Schuck Longview, along with a small group of other dedicated Unitarian Universalist feminists, crafted a resolution that, they said, would initiate "a search within the Unitarian Universalist Association for the religious roots of sexism." They brought the resolution to the 1977 General Assembly in Ithaca, New York, where it was unanimously adopted as the Women and Religion Resolution (see Appendix B).

The resolution referred to the then-existing principles of the Association, which "affirm, defend, and promote the supreme worth and dignity of every human personality, and the use of the democratic method in human relationships." It acknowledged that great strides had been taken to affirm this principle. Nevertheless, it asserted that some models of human relationship, arising out of religious myth and other teachings, still created and perpetuated attitudes that cause women everywhere to be overlooked and undervalued. It asked that Unitarian Universalists examine their religious beliefs and the extent to which those beliefs influence gender role stereotypes within their own families. It further called upon the Unitarian Universalist Association Board of Trustees, its officers and staff, and leaders and teachers throughout the movement, to "put traditional assumptions and language in perspective and to avoid sexist assumptions and language in the future."

Lucile Schuck Longview wrote about herself and her mission in *Sacred Dimensions of Women's Experience*:

> I think of myself now as "Crone Longview," named "Longview" by my unconscious nine years ago surprisingly but appropriately (because I consider myself a futurist). The term "Crone" claims the wisdom gained from experience in a long life. Each day I enjoy knowing the person I am becoming in this latest sense-of-self. I am caught up in the sacred task of undermining patriarchy. This involves taking apart and examining the threads of the intellectual cocoon into which I have been acculturated and then constructing a more life-giving and life-sustaining world view, a new consciousness that includes a revised sense of the sacred.

It was the Women and Religion Resolution and its implementation that provided the original impetus for revising the UUA Principles and Purposes. Two years after the adoption of the Women and Religion Resolution, a conference was held at the Grailville Conference Center in Loveland, Ohio. Seventy-two women attended the conference, called to carry out the mission of the resolution by organizing Women and Religion activities in the many districts of the Association. The conference was called, "Beyond This Time: A Continental Conference on Women in Religion."

Lucile Schuck Longview again came forward. She presented a workshop at the Grailville conference called, "The UUA Principles: Do They Affirm Us As Women?" The answer from the participants was a resounding "No!" Not only do those principles not affirm us as women, they said, but they fail to indicate a respect for the wholeness of life and for the earth. The Grailville conference participants set to work to revise the UUA Principles.

After further revision at the Women and Religion Coalition Convocation in East Lansing, Michigan, in 1980, an amendment to the UUA Bylaws—a proposed revision of the UUA Principles and Purposes—was sent to the districts and congregations for their consideration. The amendment was officially sponsored by five districts and fourteen congregations. Those sponsoring actions placed the amendment on the agenda of the 1981 General Assembly to be held in Philadelphia.

The amendment sent to Philadelphia (see Appendix C) replaced such terms as "foundation" and "fellowship" in the existing principles with "center" and "community." "Foundation," it was said, has hierarchical connotations and suggests a process of building that can go only up.

"Center," on the other hand, connotes heart and expansion in all directions. Though many Unitarian Universalist congregations had (and have) "fellowship" in their names, the Grailville conference objected to the term and replaced it with "community," a more encompassing and contemporary word.

A new section (f) reflected the conference's concern that the existing principles did not indicate a valuing of the wholeness of life and of the earth. The amendment called upon Unitarian Universalists to "acknowledge our responsibility to cherish the earth and its resources."

By far the most controversial revision in the proposed amendment was in the section where the existing principles spoke of the great religious teachings as "immemorially summarized in the Judeo-Christian heritage as love to God and love to humankind." The proposed revision stated that the Unitarian Universalist Association shall "Recognize our Judeo-Christian heritage as well as other traditions and seek lasting values and new insights. . . ." Several newspapers and at least one news magazine proclaimed that "the Unitarians [sic]" were proposing to remove God from their bylaws. In defense, the makers of the amendment argued that when the attempt is made to sum up Judeo-Christian and other traditions as "love to God and love to humankind" the different expressions and sensitivities of others are being denied. This rationale did not mollify the more traditional Unitarian Universalist clergy and congregations, nor did it reassure those who were convinced that this amendment—particularly the "God issue"—would tear the Association apart.

Nevertheless, the final agenda, including the proposed amendment, for the 1981 General Assembly in Philadelphia was mailed to all congregations in the spring of that year. There was immediate alarm in several quarters and swift reaction. The Reverend Carl Scovel, minister of King's Chapel in Boston and a prominent Unitarian Universalist Christian leader, wrote in a letter to all Unitarian Universalist ministers: "The impending debate on whether or not to amend [the UUA Principles] so as to eliminate the word 'God' has every prospect of becoming the kind of contest in which, regardless of who wins, our Association will lose. . . ." He went on to say that certain realities in the Unitarian Universalist Association must be recognized. He asserted that three major theological positions exist within the Association: theist, humanist, and Christian (with permutations of each). Each of these positions, Scovel said, is rooted in our common history and each has its rightful place among us. No proponent of any position, Scovel said, can presume to speak authoritatively for another. What is needed, the letter continued—and what has been neglected as a task of the Association—is a dialogue among the different positions. In short, said Scovel, "We believe that it is time to recognize and empower that pluralism which we are." The letter went on to recommend that the amendment be defeated and that a committee be appointed by the Association's Board of Trustees to study the issues. The letter, signed by twenty-five ministers, eventually attracted the signatures of over one hundred and fifty ministers. The proposed amendment was in trouble.

Opposition came from another, equally significant quarter. Members of the Board of Trustees of the Unitarian Universalist Women's Federation were greatly alarmed when the proposed amendment appeared in the final agenda. The Women's Federation leadership felt that the amendment was inimical to most Unitarian Universalist Christians and that it was more radical in its scope than most delegates to the General Assembly would support. Denise Davidoff, who became president of the Women's Federation in 1981 at the Philadelphia Assembly, said "It didn't have a prayer of passage."

Many in opposition to the proposed amendment, however, had not been intent on a win-lose outcome. They shared the conviction of the Women and Religion Committee and other proponents of the amendment that the time for revising the principles had indeed come. The Scovel letter called for the formation of a committee to study the principles. The Women's Federation also believed that, although the amendment brought to the Assembly should not be adopted, it should be heeded as a clear and just summons for significant change.

The calls for action coming from many quarters were summed up in a document distributed at the Assembly by the Reverend George "Kim" Beach. It said that although the proposed amendment was not the way to go, "We need . . . a strong statement of the 'Principles'—one with religious integrity, intellectual coherence, and literary quality. That will demand serious reflection, the gathering of ideas from all who are concerned, conceptualization and composition—such as only a small, talented group can do."

A coalition was formed with the goal of crafting a motion to refer the question of amending the principles to a committee. The coalition consisted of representatives of the Women's Federation; the Women and Religion Committee; several ministers, including Carl Scovel and Kim Beach; and youth delegates to the Assembly. The coalition framed the resolution calling for the formation of a committee to recommend new principles and purposes for the Association.

When the coalition's motion came to the floor of the Philadelphia Assembly, Denise Davidoff spoke in favor. She astutely linked the action to be taken directly to the Women and Religion Resolution. "The undertaking coincides well," she said, "with the charge given to the Women and Religion Committee to stimulate and enable an examination of our beliefs and practices to see how they create and perpetuate attitudes among us that devalue and overlook the personhood of women." Davidoff's statement was designed to reach out to those women who had brought the doomed amendment to the Assembly by aligning the "refer to committee" motion to the same Women and Religion Resolution on which that proposed amendment had been built.

The attempt at reconciliation was not entirely successful. Considerable suspicion about what might have gone on behind the scenes was expressed. There were several conspiracy theories. Some women believed a deliberate attempt had been made to disempower them. Some Unitarian Universalist Christians were convinced there had been an attempt to write them out of the Association. Many could not understand why the amendment brought to the General Assembly could not have been acted upon. To many delegates, the change in direction was sudden and inexplicable. Later, looking back to this 1981 event while addressing the General Assembly of 1984, Denise Davidoff referred to the Philadelphia Assembly as a time of "profound, searing, and long-lived conflict."

Nevertheless, the General Assembly delegates voted, by more than the required two thirds majority, "to refer proposed bylaw amendments to a committee of seven persons to be appointed by the UUA Board of Trustees." The motion charged the committee to devise and implement a process to involve the congregations and associated organizations of the Association in a reexamination of the principles and purposes as found in the current bylaws. The committee was to report to the 1982 General Assembly and to provide opportunity at that time for discussion. Following that stage of the process, the committee was charged to recommend bylaw changes that would be based on suggestions and recommendations received. The bylaw changes were to then be submitted to the congregations and organizations for study and response. Finally, recommendations for a new or revised bylaw, Purposes and Principles, were to be submitted for General Assembly action in 1983 or 1984.

The amendment created by the delegates to the Women and Religion Conference at Grailville did not prevail. It is quite clear, however, that the intent of that amendment—to carry out the mandate of the Women and Religion Resolution—was fully recognized and honored by the 1981 General Assembly at Philadelphia. It is also quite clear that the mission now to be carried forward had been established by the women of Unitarian Universalism.

Immediately after the 1981 General Assembly, the UUA Board of Trustees appointed a committee to carry out the resolution. The committee consisted of the Reverend John Cummins (Chair), Peter Fleck, the Reverend Harry Hoehler, Priscilla Ledbury, Wade McCree, the Reverend Diane Miller, and the Reverend Linnea Pearson. John Cummins resigned almost immediately, citing the pressure of other work. He also said that the Association's president had bent so far backward to recommend a diverse group for the committee that he doubted the members could work together efficiently and effectively. Cummins was replaced by the Reverend Walter Royal Jones. The committee membership changed during the three-year process to follow, but Jones guided the project to fruition with consistent patience, wisdom, and sound judgment. The committee also retained its balance of ministers and laypeople, women and men.

The committee distributed questionnaires to all Unitarian Universalist congregations, and then devoted months of long meetings and telephone conferences to sift through them. In addition to the questionnaire responses, as might be expected, they received suggestions, criticisms, and demands from all quarters. The task was summed up by committee chair Walter Royal Jones as "trying to simmer out the major areas of agreement and fashion them somehow into a set of statements that might meet with assent."

Finally, a model amendment to Article II, Section C 2.1 and C 2.2, the Purposes and Principles, emerged from the mountains of material and hours of debate and was presented to the 1983 General Assembly in Vancouver for discussion (see Appendix D). A cover letter accompanying the model amendment was something of an apology for the lack of theological specificity. It stated at the outset that the reader would not find any statements of common religious belief. The letter also justified the lack of specificity by emphasizing the broad diversity of theological and philosophical positions and "in-between positions" represented in the Association.

The movement toward pluralism in the denomination, the committee said, made it increasingly difficult to find language describing "the shrinking common denominator" of the various positions. What is shared, the letter concluded, and what the model expresses, is not so much religious belief as ethical principle.

Reaction to the model amendment was mixed. Some thought it "bloodless" and "boring." Kim Beach drafted and proposed a more poetic and liturgical format of the principles. A letter incorporating that text was given to the General Assembly delegates, requesting signatures. Although almost two hundred delegates signed the letter forwarded to the committee, the members believed it necessary to stay with the two-year voting process established in the bylaws.

The committee had formulated seven principles, each preceded by a statement that, within their diversity, the Unitarian Universalist societies would "affirm and promote." In general, the proposed principles were received well by the Vancouver delegates. The committee members returned to their meetings and conversations to polish their model amendment for preliminary and final approval at the 1984 and 1985 General Assemblies.

Before presenting the amendment to the 1984 General Assembly in Columbus, Ohio, for preliminary approval, the committee made two major changes to the model presented in Vancouver. First of all, as a way of addressing the painful divisions that had surfaced at the

General Assembly in Philadelphia, the committee separated the principles into two sections, the "principles" and the "sources."

Addressing the issue of diversity, the committee stated in the "sources" section that, although we are indeed diverse, what we share is a "living tradition." That living tradition draws from many sources. Among the sources included are direct experience, the words and deeds of prophetic men and women, humanist teachings and—taking again the hands of the Christian Unitarian Universalists—"Jewish and Christian teachings which call us to respond to God's love by loving our neighbors as ourselves."

The second significant change made by the committee was to completely revise the historic order of the principles. The change in order expressed a changing focus from the place of the individual, her and his "inherent worth and dignity," to the expanding context of community, earth, and universe, "respect for the integrity of the earth and its resources."

Much of the fine-tuning, the final phrasing, was done at the very last meeting. In a letter to this writer, Walter Royal Jones Jr. says, "What was most significant for me was the synergy of the later sessions where we literally rearranged almost everything we had done . . . things suddenly seemed to fall into place . . . our materials were ceasing to be a grab-bag collection; they were defining a form of their own." If that is too much of the mythic muse for some, there should be no doubt that the committee's work had been solid and deliberate from beginning to end. As Jones wrote, "Behind us lay the full three years' dialogue with the churches and with each other." Behind them, too, lay almost six years of process since that small group of women met with Lucile Schuck Longview in Lexington, Massachusetts.

The motion to revise the bylaws of the Unitarian Universalist Association with new purposes and principles went to the 1984 General Assembly in Columbus, Ohio, for preliminary approval. Needless to say, several amendments to the motion were offered on the floor. Three of the amendments were adopted and were incorporated into the final wording.

The word "liberty" was added to the sixth principle, making it ". . . with peace, liberty, and justice for all." The seventh principle was amended, on a motion by the Reverend Paul L'Herrou, from "respect for Earth and interdependence of its living systems" to the version that has now stood the test of time, "respect for the interdependent web of all existence of which we are a part." This inspired language, with the first principle to affirm and promote "the inherent worth and dignity of every person," truly framed the principles as a whole.

An amendment to the sources section added "wisdom from the world's religions" to the traditions. (Eleven years later, another source was added, largely through the efforts of members of The Covenant of Unitarian Universalist Pagans. The source is described as "spiritual teachings of earth-centered traditions which celebrate the sacred circle of life and instruct us to live in harmony with the rhythms of nature." Almost as much controversy attended this amendment as occurred in 1984. Many felt that "earth-centered traditions" were included in the seventh principle and in the world religions references. Less academic objections included characterizing the amendment proposers as witches.

Nevertheless, the "earth-centered traditions" amendment passed by a vote of 735 to 358—a narrow margin of the two-thirds majority required for a change in bylaws. Following the vote, a Crow Indian delegate, in full native dress, rose to declare that he was a Unitarian Universalist and that the Assembly had voted to include his heritage.

This later scene was reminiscent of the 1985 General Assembly in Atlanta, Georgia, when Section C 2.1 and Section C 2.2 of the Unitarian Universalist Association Bylaws were finally amended to loud applause, sighs of relief, tears, and a few shrugs of "wait and see."

In 1987, ten years after the Women and Religion Resolution was adopted, Lucile Schuck Longview wrote, "Because of the new Principles, we are at a *new beginning. . . .*" We labor in a new field—in a new paradigm—a new reality construct. We must lift up and celebrate the fact that a phenomenal change in practice and in ideology has been embraced by the Unitarian Universalist Association." ("Because of the New Principles," a paper delivered at the Joseph Priestley District on June 6, 1987.)

—EAF

The Inherent Worth and Dignity of Every Person

MARILYN SEWELL

The first principle is our foundation. It speaks of respecting others enough to never objectify and control them in the service of ideology, however precious. It encourages people to unfold according to their true and authentic nature, to live with integrity according to their own heart's leaning. As Unitarian Universalists, we do not ask members to adopt any creed or doctrine. People are accepted as they are, whether they are Christians, Buddhists, Jews, humanists, atheists, or simply searching. Whether they are straight, gay, lesbian, bisexual, or transgendered. Whether they are socialists or Republicans. Whether they are white or people of color. All have worth and dignity. All are welcome at the table.

The first principle is human-centered. It implies that living on this earth is the proper focus of our time and attention. Heaven will take care of itself. "One world at a time," as Thoreau said. Furthermore, our first principle strongly implies that we are called to create justice where justice now does not exist. If all people do have worth and dignity, can we allow some of them to live with no hope? To allow people to go hungry and without shelter? To turn our eyes away from discrimination?

Perhaps it might be useful at this point to reflect on the historical antecedents to the first principle. Unitarianism was born out of the left wing of the Protestant Reformation. The Reformation itself was, of course, the child of the Renaissance, that great social, cultural, and religious revolution that over several centuries changed the way humans perceived the world and themselves in it. Beginning in Italy as early as the fourteenth century, scholars such as Giorgio Biandrata began to question received knowledge. This spirit of inquiry spread rapidly throughout Europe. Classical learning was revived. People began to see the human being as having beauty, dignity, and perfectibility.

The Reformation was a kind of biblical renaissance, or a return to the source, the scripture, rather than a blind adherence to authority. Our piece of it began in Poland in 1579. A man named Faustus Socinus published a tract in Racow that promoted the concept of Jesus as a man chosen by God, but not himself God. Socinus's position denied the Trinity as put forward by the early Christian church at the Council of Nicea in 325 CE. His followers, called Socinians, worshiped in Poland until 1658 when they were banned by the Polish legislature. Many found refuge in the Unitarian community in Transylvania, where King John Sigismund (our only Unitarian king!) allowed diversity of religious belief and signed the first edict of religious freedom in the Western world. One should keep in mind that this was an extremely unusual position to take, considering that at this time people were still being burned at the stake for heresy.

In the eighteenth century, this free faith spread to England and hence to the United States at the end of that century. A defining moment came in our country when our most prominent minister, William Ellery Channing, preached his sermon "Unitarian Christianity" in Baltimore in 1819 (called the Baltimore Sermon). Channing made four major points: (1) that the Bible was open to question and criticism, (2) that the concept of the Trinity was invalid, (3) that Jesus was human and not God, and (4) that God is infinitely good and not a God of wrath.

Universalism emerged from seventeenth-century Germany and England and spread to the United States about the same time as Unitarianism. The liberal theology of the Universalists was similar to that of the Unitarians. They were known for their compassion and tolerance, in particular. And they believed that everyone would be saved, a remarkable heresy, considering the hell-fire message of the Great Awakening preachers in our country during the eighteenth and nineteenth centuries. The two denominations merged in 1961.

Although the roots of Unitarian Universalism are Judeo-Christian, our insistence on the primacy of conscience has drawn adherents of diverse religious beliefs, including agnostics and atheists. Believing that all people have spiritual needs, we invite whoever would come, asking only that people give the same respect and tolerance to others that they would want for themselves.

We are a free religious faith. Because of this radical respect for others and their choices, Unitarian Universalists are able to act as advocates for certain oppressed groups when other denominations would find such action politically impossible. For example, in 1993 when Ballot Measure 9 threatened the civil rights of gays and lesbians in Oregon, our church in Portland acted swiftly, with no debate. We made a very public witness by wrapping our entire block with a red ribbon and declaring ourselves a "Hate-Free Zone."

Another congregation a few blocks away could not take such a public stand, though the minister of that church let his flock know that he was against Ballot Measure 9. The church was greatly divided on the issue, but they did not make any public statement. I was thankful for our religious history and tradition that let us declare openly that everyone has worth and dignity, and everyone must be treated equally under the law.

What is the theological grounding of our first principle? Because we believe that our God is one God, one and the same spirit of love uniting all people, then all are brothers and sisters. I am reminded of Dr. Norbert Capek's prayer at the first flower communion service in his church in Czechoslovakia on June 4, 1923: "Let us renew our resolution sincerely to be real brothers and sisters regardless of any kind of bar which estranges. . . . In this holy resolution may we be strengthened knowing that we are God's family; that one spirit, the spirit of love, unites us. . . ."

Capek lived his theology. He became a leader of Nazi resistance during World War II, helping Czechs escape the Gestapo, and speaking in his sermons ever more directly about the abuses of the Nazis towards Jews, gays, gypsies, and the disabled. He was arrested for listening to British radio and sent to prison. Though he won his case at trial, his release was opposed by the Nazis, and he was transferred to Dachau, where he died in Nazi medical experiments. Capek came out of a religious tradition that saw all as having worth and dignity, that all were united in the spirit of God's unconditional love. He saw that we all must try to love as God loves, and he was so deeply imbued with this value that he was willing to die for it.

Though our first principle is the foundation of our theological and relational lives in community, we must acknowledge that there are questions and contradictions that plague us. One of these questions emerges in regard to the tolerance we profess. Some Unitarian Universalists who have moved away from Christianity, but who have not yet resolved the painful experiences of their childhood faith, find it difficult to tolerate Christian Unitarian Universalists, or even the use of the Bible in a worship service. Some Unitarian Universalists are intolerant of politically conservative individuals and discourage their participation in our churches. When we reject individuals because we disagree with their perspective on religion or politics, we are violating our first principle. "We need not think alike to love alike," wrote Francis Dávid, an early martyr. Our tradition pledges us to be deeply respectful of others, even when we cannot accept their values or theological perspectives.

On the other hand, in the name of radical respect, sometimes we find ourselves being foolishly tolerant of individual behavior that should not be accepted because it is destructive of the larger community. Some churches allow unhealthy individuals to exert extraordinary influence in the life of the church body because members want to always appear "open" and "loving." This tolerance of harmful behavior is not consistent with our principles, for it is in violation of the law of love and healthy respect for the larger community.

An example can be drawn from an experience in the congregation I serve. A known date rapist started visiting, trying to connect with various women during the coffee hour. Women were being warned surreptitiously, but nobody was questioning the man's "right" to visit our church and prey on the women there. But our church is private property, and anyone who comes there to harm others loses his privilege of fellowship with us, to my way of thinking. I asked several of our largest men to surround him and give him the following message, "We know why you are here. We want you to leave and never come back. If you do, we will call the police." Some people questioned my action as "heavy-handed." After all, he had committed no crime on our premises. My perspective is that, yes, this man has worth and dignity—and, no, it doesn't follow that we should tolerate his harmful behavior.

And what do we do when contradictions appear? For example, most Unitarian Universalists believe in the right of a woman to determine whether or not she will carry a baby to term. But if each life has "inherent worth and dignity," what about a woman's decision to abort a fetus that is found to have Down's Syndrome? Though we claim that every life has worth and dignity, many Unitarian Universalists join the approximately eighty percent of

Americans who believe in the death penalty, somehow concluding that committing heinous crimes makes a human being lose human status. We have passed a resolution on the right to die and we speak of "death with dignity," but when we look at how doctor-assisted suicide has shifted to include nonvoluntary euthanasia in the Netherlands, what does that knowledge imply about potential abuse of our first principle?

We are called upon to reject the easy answers and to struggle with the values and conflicts inherent in human life. We must study and reflect and think and write and get beneath the surface of things, or else we will become facile in regard to these significant moral and ethical issues.

As liberal religious people, the fruits of the spirit must be made manifest in our commitment to justice. We are sometimes better at articulating our commitment than actually carrying out any action. As one wag said, "We think because we've said it, we've done it." Nowhere is this truer than in our class consciousness. We tend to think of ourselves as a people set apart, just a notch or two better than others. We are middle class and upper middle class, with a vengeance: A middle-class person of color would have a relatively easy time moving into one of our congregations, compared to someone who has working class assumptions.

It should be said as well that we are by and large a prosperous bunch. Though we say we would not like to see anyone lacking food or medical care, the truth is that the startlingly garish financial inequities of our day do not seem to compel our attention as a people. Perhaps this is because we are comfortable ourselves and cannot always relate to the poverty of others. Perhaps it is because a large percentage of us own stock in the large corporations that exercise so much control over our government and therefore over how the economic pie is split. Again, we must monitor our actions to see that they fit our words. Should there not be a fit, our words will ring hollow.

"We believe in the inherent worth and dignity of all persons." Imperfect as we are, this principle calls us into right relationship with others. It calls for profound respect, even when we differ with the views and behavior of another. It calls for gentleness and forgiveness and the understanding that redemption is just a decision away. It calls us to leave the safety and sameness of our suburbs and stand against hunger and hopelessness in our urban streets. Our first principle remains a touchstone out of our remarkable tradition, a covenant of relationship that supports the other principles and orients us remarkably quickly when we lose our way.

Justice, Equity, and Compassion in Human Relations

RICHARD S. GILBERT

Justice, equity, and compassion are lived values of a free faith, suggesting that the spiritual life must express itself ethically. Church historian Earl Morse Wilbur gives us a powerful example of the seriousness with which one of our Unitarian Universalist antecedents—the sixteenth-century Minor Church of Poland—took that imperative. The Minor Church's theology was Socinianism, after Faustus Socinus who believed that Jesus saved, not by his death on the cross, but by the persuasive power of his life on earth. To an impressive degree the church stressed church covenant—not only mutual promises and account-ability to one another within the community, but their responsibilities to those outside the community. Its atten-tion was centered less on doctrine than on the practical applications of religious principles to daily life. Historian David Parke wrote, "Its most notable social practice was that of love and tolerance in human relations" (*The Epic of Unitarianism*).

Adherents were evaluated on those responsibilities four times a year just before the celebration of the Lord's Supper. To prepare for this solemn communion, the congregation met Saturday for worship and to confess their sins. Congregants were interviewed privately about their conduct for the period just passed, taken to task for their faults, and urged to repent of their evil ways. Evidently this regular self-examination and social accountability were taken very seriously by all involved and helped maintain a high standard of conduct. So impressive was this spiritual and ethical discipline that even those who most disagreed with its doctrines were impressed by the Minor Church. Earl Morse Wilbur reported that a Catholic historian declared this group constituted "the most influential page in Polish religious history, and one reason why its adherents did not become more numerous was that its moral demands were too strict" (*A History of Unitarianism: Socinianism and Its Antecedents*).

These words are reminiscent of the more recent question of Unitarian Universalist minister Harry Meserve, "If you were arrested for being a Unitarian Universalist, would there be enough evidence to convict you?" Unitarian Universalism has always emphasized deed over creed— as Ralph Waldo Emerson put it, somewhat bluntly, "what you are . . . thunders so that I cannot hear what you say . . ." (*Letters and Social Aims*).

Indicative of this emphasis is a 1981 story that appeared in the *Chicago Tribune* about Mother Theresa and then president of the Unitarian Universalist Association, Eugene Pickett. During a visit to Chicago she was asked the question of life's final meaning. Her answer was, "To become holy, and to go to Heaven." Eugene Pickett's response to the same question was a significant variant of that theme, "The purpose of life is to become whole, and to create a Heaven on earth."

The very name Unitarian Universalist suggests a strong ethical component. "Unitarian" implies the unity of all beings, binding us together in one human family. "Universalist" suggests that our concerns are global in nature—no one is to be excluded. Affirming and promoting "justice, equity, and compassion in human relations" articulates that tradition.

I understand religion to be that core of ultimate meanings and values out of which we live our lives. Central to the meaning of being a Unitarian Universalist is to be for others—commitment to the service of life is a key expression of being a spiritual and ethical human being. I sum up my central religious conviction in these words: In the love of beauty and the spirit of truth, we unite for the celebration of life and the service of humanity.

Compassion

Compassion is the spiritual value that undergirds Unitarian Universalist ethics. Living compassionately is an act of thanksgiving, flowing from the blessings of life that we wish to share. The overflow of that compassion in the individual leads to the quest for equity and justice. As former Unitarian Universalist Association President William Schulz wrote in the *World* magazine, "Spirituality is the inspiration for all politics which redeems. For once I have looked on the abundance of creation, I cannot rest while others, caught up in its flaws, are deprived of the view." More succinctly put by theologian Gene Reeves, "to be is to be for others."

Compassion comes from the Latin *com*, meaning "together," and *pati*, meaning "to suffer"—to suffer together. In German the word is *mitleid*—feeling the misfortune of the other. There are times when our only response to another's pain is to share it. "Sorrow shared is sorrow halved," as an old German saying puts it. Unitarian Universalists seek to create caring communities in their congregations, a mutual ministry in grappling with life's vicissitudes. We realize that none of us can navigate life's treacherous waters alone.

Often our liberal religious tendency has been toward social reform rather than pastoral care, as if the two were unrelated. It is true that in our fundamental finitude we bump up against the humanly unfixable, that which is built into the very nature of things and cannot be changed. Often suffering simply comes from the burdens of life and death, and there is nothing to do but accept our fate gracefully and try to nurture others similarly afflicted.

The striking thing about conceptions of compassion is that this feeling of deep sympathy and sorrow for another who is stricken by suffering is accompanied by a strong desire to alleviate the pain or remove its cause. Sympathy—feeling pity—turns into empathy—feeling with—and finally issues in action to serve the needs of the neighbor.

In 1954 Kenneth Clark argued the case for public school integration before the US Supreme Court in the historic *Brown v. Board of Education* decision. Clark subsequently critiqued the possibility of academic objectivity by asking the arresting question, "How is it possible to study a slum objectively?" By extrapolation, how can we presume to understand our society without deep feelings of moral outrage at the pervasiveness of suffering and injustice?

Clark's question was anticipated by Margaret Sanger, founder of the planned parenthood movement. She was a public health nurse who day after day visited scenes of suffering in which poor women were plunged into even greater despair with unwanted pregnancies. "These were not merely 'unfortunate conditions among the poor' such as we read about. I knew the women personally. They were living, breathing, human beings, with hopes, fears, and aspirations like my own." Sanger told the story of Mrs. Sachs, a twenty-eight-year-old woman with septicemia as a result of a self-induced abortion. The woman's doctor warned her that one more pregnancy could be fatal. She begged the doctor to tell her what she could do to avoid the pregnancy. The doctor said, "Tell Jake to sleep on the roof." Mrs. Sachs begged Margaret Sanger, "Please tell me the secret, and I'll never breathe it to a soul." Sanger was haunted by the request, but did nothing. Three months later Mrs. Sachs was pregnant again, went into a coma and died. Sanger left the deathbed scene and walked the streets. That night she decided that she could not go on like this, merely a witness to human suffering. "I was resolved to seek out the root of evil, to do something to change the destiny of mothers whose miseries were vast as the sky." The planned parenthood movement is the social action that grew out of her compassion for one suffering soul.

David Rhys Williams, a Unitarian Universalist minister who combined the prophetic and the pastoral, articulated this sense of compassion when he wrote, "We are joined together by a mystic oneness whose source we may never know, but whose reality we can never doubt. . . . We are our neighbor's keeper, because that neighbor is but our larger self. . . . Behold, thou shalt love thy neighbor as thyself, because thy neighbor is thyself" ("Thy Neighbor Is Thyself" in *We Sing of Life with We Speak of Life*).

Equity

Nineteenth-century Unitarian Senator Charles Sumner once said, "There are dinners without appetites at one end of the table and appetites without dinners at the other." In that graphic image he captured the concept of inequity—fundamental unfairness in the distribution of goods necessary for life. Some people have too much and don't know what to do with it; some people have too little and don't know how to get enough. Equity ought to be distinguished from equality with its presumption of sameness. Equity carries the sense of fairness, not identity, fairness being a value intuitively grasped by children at an early age.

In his dinner table image, Sumner grasped the reality of a world of plenty in which superfluity and want stand side by side both within and among nations. Equity not only demands that a society improve the conditions of its impoverished, but also calls into question the corruptions of its affluent. Lord Acton's famous dictum on the corrupting potential of power could thus be translated, "Affluence tends to corrupt; absolute affluence corrupts absolutely." If we believe that religious values should determine how the marketplace operates rather than the other way around, equity becomes a measuring rod for social justice.

There is little ethical question that we ought to treat people fairly without regard to race, creed, gender, affectional orientation, or physical or mental ability. However, what is equitable in the economic sphere is a much more debatable point.

Imagine you are at a gathering that is to create a new society. You are among rational people with roughly similar needs and interests. Generally speaking, you are equal in terms of power and ability so that none is able to dominate the others. You are to make your decisions on the basis of enlightened self-interest. At the same time, you wish to establish the economic guidelines for a truly just social order.

You live behind a "veil of ignorance," not knowing how well you will fare in this new social environment. There is an equal chance you will succeed or fail—that you will become the most or the least affluent in the group. The annual income available to you is $200,000. There are ten "work positions" (from welfare recipient to CEO) that are necessary to maintain this society. Allocate the income as fairly as possible. After you have made your allocations, draw a slip of paper that will indicate your "work position" and income. How equitable would you make your new society? How would fairness look?

There is a creative tension here between absolute equality and equity as fairness. Although most would not say that each person deserved exactly equal resources, how does one allocate these resources in a free society? What criteria are to be used? It has been suggested that fairness is realized when inequality works to help the least able to compete in the society's marketplace. There is no formula here, but religious prophets through the ages have excoriated extremes of wealth and poverty—denounced the rich for their indifference to the poor, and have generally chosen what has been called "a preferential option for the poor."

Justice

A *New Yorker* cartoon depicts our dilemma: It shows three fish swimming, one behind the other. First is a small fish saying, "There is no justice." Immediately behind, ready to swallow it, is a larger fish saying, "There is some justice in the world." Finally, there is a large fish about to swallow both saying, "The world is just."

"Justice is love operating at a distance," said theologian Joseph Sittler. While compassionate love is a personal moral value, justice generally deals with larger social contexts. It implies a fair distribution of social benefits and burdens. Justice allocates resources based on need, not greed.

Justice, properly understood, is systemic, aiming at the underlying causes of social problems, not at their symptoms. Treating symptoms alone might well be a soporific to cover fundamental injustice; it is like putting Band-Aids on a cancer. Thus, food kitchens, however laudable, merely feed the victims of a fundamentally unjust social order instead of rooting out causes of hunger. A systemic approach challenges the underlying premises and workings of economies that produce "poverty in the midst of plenty." A systemic approach deals with policy issues, taxation, government welfare programs, and income distribution.

Systemic change contrasts with attitudinal change as the most effective way to achieve social justice. In the latter it is assumed that one must first work on individual attitudes before behavior can be modified. ("You can't legislate morality!") This is the philosophy in which social change consists of bringing people to Christ; social amelioration automatically follows. In liberal circles, it is sometimes assumed this transformation comes through "consciousness raising," as if awareness of problems, proper attitudes toward them and good intentions somehow inexorably lead to their solution.

Nineteenth-century Unitarian minister Theodore Parker put it graphically in his book *Theodore Parker's Experience as a Minister*: "Yet it seemed to me the money given by public and private charity—two fountains that never fail in Puritanic Boston—was more than sufficient to relieve it all, and gradually remove the deep-seated and unseen cause which, in the hurry of business and of money, is not attended to. There is a hole in the dim-lit public bridge, where many fall through and perish. Our mercy pulls a few out of the water; it does not stop the hole, nor light the bridge, nor warn men of the peril! We need the great Charity that palliates effects of wrong, and the greater Justice which removes the Cause."

Whereas democracy enables decisions by majority vote and whereas the market allocates resources by what has been called "the invisible hand," justice is a virtue that transcends these instrumental ways of making decisions. For example, while democratic voting and the medical marketplace leave millions of people without proper health care, justice requires that basic health care needs of all people be met. Justice is like the carpenter's plumb line that the prophet Amos likened to divine righteousness as the criterion for all human endeavors. The vertical line (justice) intersects the horizontal line (society). Justice can be determined neither by democratic vote nor market machination. It is a transcendent human value that judges all such arrangements.

The Beloved Community

While traditional Judaism and Christianity refer to the coming of the Kingdom of God as the end point of human destiny, the term Beloved Community better elucidates the liberal religious concern for compassion, equity, and justice. Community is a term both contemporary and democratic, while kingdom is royalist and anachronistic. Kingdom also connotes male power in a sexist universe, while community brings a sense of gender equity. God is a term that is variously interpreted by Unitarian Universalists and probably will never yield to common understanding. Beloved Community is a term for humanistic, theistic, and other theological perspectives. And the term

Beloved Community implies that ours is a project in loving the neighbor near and distant, an endeavor that is squarely in humanity's hands—keeping in step with the long Unitarian Universalist tradition of trying to build a heaven on earth.

The Beloved Community, then, is a constellation of values to be lived out by the individual and the religious community in the wider society. Unitarian Universalism seeks to be a "church without walls" in which social concerns become the agenda of the people as they take their spiritual and ethical values into the public arena. Our congregations seek to become communities of moral discourse and social action on the frontiers of living, teaching their children by what they are and do. The congregants become conspirators for the Beloved Community—conspiracy meaning "to breathe together." There is, then, in Unitarian Universalism a seamless garment of spirituality and social action; we are a "spiritual center with a civic circumference." Faith exists by mission.

As Unitarian Universalists with a proud history of repairing the world, we cannot be content to be mere occupants of time and space. We want our time on earth to mean something; we want the space in which we live and move and have our being to be in good repair. We are ill content to wear our religion only in our heads and hearts; we want it to be expressed with our hands. Social justice work is not simply another option on the spiritual menu, an "add on" extracurricular activity, but part and parcel of what it means to be a Unitarian Universalist.

The Prophetic Imperative

Unitarian Universalism lives under what I call a "prophetic imperative" to work for the Beloved Community. The term prophetic here does not refer to predicting the future, but to the biblical prophets who spoke truth to power, who understood themselves and their communities to be under a divine mandate to live out compassion, equity, and justice in communal life. Although we are not as clear as they were that God has whispered the truth in our ears, we are clear that there are values that are not optional—that must be lived.

In a 1970 *Harper's Magazine* review of Joseph Heller's play, *We Bombed in New Haven*, critic Walter Kerr describes one rather unsettling Broadway evening that the play's star Jason Robards experienced. He was playing an Air Force captain whose duty it was to send pilots to their probable deaths during the Vietnam War. The play provided two actor-audience intimacies, suggesting that an actor is not merely an actor or a character in a play, but a flesh and blood human being.

One evening Robards finished the scene with his usual bitter discouragement, and began his exit to give his fateful orders and make way for subsequent scenes, when a small group from the audience left their seats, proceeded down the aisle and summoned him back to the footlights. These unexpected activists told him that at least they were not going to permit the fighting to continue.

Kerr continues, "Apparently Mr. Robards, who at least wanted the play to continue, tried gentle persuasion, urging the interlopers to return to their seats quietly. They wouldn't. They'd been invited to protest and they were protesting. If the way to stop war was to stop this play, they would do it. That's what the play had been asking them to do all along, wasn't it?" The protesters refused to heed Robards's plea that the play be allowed to go on, until he lost his patience and exclaimed, "What do you want me to do? I'm only an actor!"

That is precisely the point. We are actors, historical actors, agents of change. If history is to veer off its suicidal courses it will only be because of actors who take time seriously, who link learning and action because they are inseparable. Joseph Heller's point was that while actors always wind up safe in their dressing rooms, people can be killed. In actual warfare there are no actors, only people.

"The second intimacy," continued Kerr, "had to do with acknowledging the fact that we, as an audience, were present at the play and could, if we wished, take a hand in it." There came a point in the play when at last Robards's character understood that all of the fictitious killing was real, and tried to stop it. However, he was informed by his commanding officer that the orders could not be questioned, and that the bloodshed must go on. The Robards character was caught up in a moral outrage that caused him to turn to the audience and say that it would not go on because we—the audience—wouldn't let it go on. We would halt the vicious cycle now that we knew.

Kerr concluded, "Mr. Heller was, of course, here using the actor-audience relationship for the purposes of irony. He assumed that we would certainly not intervene on Mr. Robards's side, that we would continue to sit there as we always do sit there, allowing war to go on as we always do allow war to go on. Our silence was to indict us, our refusal to act in the theater was to become our refusal to act in life."

To refuse to act in life is to abdicate our role as spiritual and moral beings. There is a vacuum in religious life when we fail to act out our values. We are then incomplete people; our growth is stifled; our lives found wanting. The spiritual impulse, far from being a check on social action, should be a spur.

Theodore Parker said that the moral arc of the universe is long, but it bends toward justice. The bending, however, is not automatic, nor is it inexorable. It is dependent on people who feel compassion, equity, and justice as imperatives of their faith.

The two basic questions we must ultimately ask are these: What should we do? and Why should we do it? We should try to repair the world because in so doing we will help to repair not only the world but ourselves as well.

That ethical imperative was well understood by our Minor Church predecessors in the sixteenth century and has been understood throughout Unitarian Universalist history. As Unitarian Universalist writer/minister Robert Fulghum puts it in *It Was on Fire When I Lay Down on It*, "I do not want your sympathy for the needs of humanity. I want your muscle. I do not want to talk about what you understand about this world. I want to know what you will do about it. I do not want to know what you hope, I want to know what you will work for."

The prophets of old could not have said it better.

Acceptance
of One Another
and Encouragement to
Spiritual Growth
in Our Congregations

CAROLYN OWEN-TOWLE

Unitarianism began when the Western world's first Edict of Religious Toleration was signed in 1558, in Transylvania. It was the work of the first and only Unitarian king in history, John Sigismund. In Eastern Europe, perilous theological wars had been waged throughout the Reformation between Catholics and Protestants. For the sake of religious harmony, the young yet sagacious king declared that everyone would henceforth freely embrace the religion and faith that they preferred and would refrain from inflicting any harm or injury upon another.

Several years later, the same king issued another Act of Religious Tolerance and Freedom of Conscience. The key line signified that "no one shall be reviled for their religion by anyone. . . ." Throughout our history this has been the underlying affirmation of Unitarianism, and later, Unitarian Universalism.

Our faith acknowledges that no two people think, believe, taste, feel, hear, or encounter life in the same way. Those who are disinclined, for whatever reason, to conform to a single commonly held creed seek their own truthful and compassionate ways to live. We give our approval and seek acceptance because it is validating. It frees us to become our best possible selves. It is our very differences that make it necessary to practice acceptance toward one another. Francis Dávid, sixteenth-century Unitarian forebear, reminded us "not to think alike, but to love alike."

But just how accepting do I have to be?

I may assert that you are a valuable person, but if I am a theist and you are an atheist do I have to accept your view? Wouldn't it just be easier to band together with other theists and let the atheists go their own way? If I find you to be full of pride and I know myself to be modest, do I have to accept your behavior? If I believe in reincarnation and you claim people simply cease to exist when they die, must I accept your view even though your thinking disturbs me? If the color of our skin is different, might I not ignore rather than make an effort to know you? If you love differently than I do, might I discount and turn you aside? If I am in a wheelchair and you are standing, do you have any obligation to accept me as a genuine and valuable person?

Living in a pluralistic society, we cannot help but pay daily attention to just what is meant by acceptance. It is within our capability to accept someone for their intrinsic worth without necessarily accepting what they believe or how they act. That, in fact, is what we are obliged by our principles to do. But, it does take a certain amount of maturity to separate being from behavior. It is a learned discipline that takes both mind and heart, looking into the person him- or herself beyond fixed categories. It means attuning to their hearts and recognizing the common humanity you share. Our empathy tells us that people are tender, fragile beings with feelings, yearnings, aspirations, and fears that are similar to our own.

We know when we are accepted. We don't earn it. We do not even find it by looking. But when it comes to us, through a remark, or an attitude, we stand a little taller and bloom a little brighter. The most difficult, yet first, task is to accept ourselves. Acceptance comes easily when we receive it from infancy. It takes intentional effort, when we have to develop it later in life. One of the best ways to begin is within an accepting religious community.

How can we grow a climate of acceptance in our Unitarian Universalist society? Here are a few suggestions:

- The first lesson is learned the day we walk through the door of a Unitarian Universalist house of worship. How the stranger is welcomed is a test of a congregation's commitment to part of our third principle, "acceptance of one another."
- Religious education is an essential venue. From the earliest days of childhood until our old age, we need to

know that we are radically accepted, that we are valuable per se, and that our ideas are worthy of respect. All religious education leaders must demonstrate genuine acceptance even as they teach it.

- Tell the story of your faith community repeatedly to give young and old alike a sense of belonging to something of transcendent worth. Describe what has and has not worked.

- Seek out religious education curricula for adults that help people develop a sense of their worth and validity.

- Begin meetings both with an inspirational thought and a check-in to encourage parishioners in getting to know one another beyond being simply the task-bearers of the church. Listen to one another for what is important to your spirits.

- When you must disagree, do so with respect. Affirm, if you can, the other congregants' right to their positions even as you differ. Apologize when you are wrong. Concentrate not on winning, but on developing understanding between people.

- Through your Social Action Committee or the Unitarian Universalist Service Committee, seek ways to open the congregation to greater diversity. Examine attitudes about racism, classism, ableism, ageism, homophobia, sexism, and other active injustices. Ask yourselves who in the congregation must hide their true selves for fear they will not be accepted, and see how you can help to change certain attitudes.

- Set limits. Honor another's position, yet insist on equal respect for yours. This will foster compromise. Acceptance is a two-way street.

If the radical notion of acceptance were to be internalized by the peoples of the world, we would have peace, and civilization would survive. As Unitarian Universalists we are called by our principles to make the practice and teaching of acceptance a lifelong commitment.

The second part of the third principle is "encouragement to spiritual growth." Ours is a hopeful faith. It holds out the promise that we can become as full, rich contributors to life as our imaginations and our efforts can take us. We have to work at it, however. Spiritual development takes effort. Every time we come from a personal rather than intellectual place we express ourselves spiritually. As Unitarian Universalist minister Mark Belletini wrote, "we sing our faith as well as argue it, we love silence as well as our words, we act in concert to bring justice to the world even as we guard our individual spirits."

If acceptance affirms us as we are, encouragement pushes us toward whom we might become. As crucial as acceptance is to our spiritual and emotional health, we need frequent nudges by others to grow lest we stagnate. Our religious community helps us grow beyond ourselves, both personally and communally.

Our covenantal faith requires us to make a vow of commitment to support and encourage one another. We realize we cannot make it alone in life. We need to invest in one another's humanity. The church calls us to make deep connections with our rich history, with fellow sojourners, and with the larger community. In the saving community, we can risk sticking our necks out with each other. And in the process we begin to become who we authentically are.

The word "encourage" literally means to put courage or heart into another. All of us need reassuring as we face the travails of life. Sometimes that lift comes in the form of a hug or a supportive comment. It might be heard in a sermon, a piece of music, or a poem. At other times it comes as a nudge to get going, to turn around, or to buck up. Whatever it is, when it comes from someone with whom we share a common quest for spiritual growth, it helps.

How am I to encourage others? What have I got to share?

Think of yourself as a mirror reflecting someone's image back to them. What do you see in them that you can affirm? Look again. It may not be apparent at first. When you notice a strength, an accomplishment, an insight— tell them, as accurately as you can. That way they will know you are being authentic, and they can accept what you have given them. We cannot run around encouraging everyone all the time. But neither should we miss an opportunity when we see it. There is too little encouragement given. The result is often discouragement. We are all pressured by time and commitments. Just getting through life becomes the goal. But, the power of encouragement cannot be underestimated. A child flourishes when encouraged. That same child will try her- or himself in new ways when given a genuine boost.

How can we foster an encouraging spiritual community? There are a number of ways. Here are a few ideas:

- We all minister to one another. Encouragement can become a cornerstone of our ministries.

- A tone is set in any group by the way in which individuals support or fail to support others. Appreciation, recognition, and thanks are caring means to encourage others. Give public recognition to volunteers and staff who have given greatly of their time and effort to the congregation or to the outside community. Recognize contributors of time and/or money.
- Worship constitutes opening the soul to encouragement. This is the optimal time to give a spiritual uplift to the congregation. The music and words, the setting and decor all contribute to or detract from a person's worship experience.
- Pay attention to the space within which you worship. Prepare ahead. Make sure it is clean, properly heated or cooled, and otherwise comfortable. Details make a big difference.
- Our children need leaders who care for and encourage them. Teach leaders the value of encouraging their youngsters, through example, story, and personal interaction.
- Begin meetings by setting a spiritual tone. Light a chalice with an inspirational thought, a song, or relate a short story. Encouraging people to share their lives, even briefly, makes them feel connected to the community and valued.
- Encourage people to try themselves at new skills through adult classes, committee work, or liturgical leadership. Praise their efforts.
- Invite individuals, one at a time, to share their credo, their affirmation of faith during worship.
- Note people who are absent from the community and write them a note or call them.

We Unitarian Universalists are charged to build a more just and loving world. The work of change and justice building is demanding of stalwart souls. Bruised by life, we need to renew our spirit of resolve, and so we look to our faith communities for strength. Here we can give and receive no greater gift than acceptance of one another for who we are and encouragement for what we might be. May we find healing in the crucial directive of the third principle.

A Free and Responsible Search for Truth and Meaning

FREDRIC MUIR

It is "a free and responsible search for truth and meaning" that has brought many through our doors. In small-group introductions, discussion groups, and private conversations, I have heard hundreds (maybe thousands) of stories that sound like this composite:

> When I left the faith of my childhood, I didn't think I needed a religion—I sure didn't need a congregation. But then, it happened—maybe it was work or finding a partner, maybe it was the kids or a change in my family—I knew something in my life was missing. There was this deep, empty place that needed filling.
>
> I started shopping for religion—some place where I could ask questions and not be told what I had to

believe. This went on for years. I can't remember if it was a friend of mine or a relative or maybe something I read in the paper, but somehow I heard about Unitarian Universalism. I still didn't come right away, but finally one Sunday I got up and said "This is it. This morning I'm going to that church." And even though I still have a lot of questions, and while the void isn't completely filled, I feel good about what I'm doing and where I'm going. I really like it here.

I've heard a version of this story many times, and it is a story I never grow tired of hearing. Perhaps it is the closest thing we have to a religious testimonial. In this sense it is a sacred story.

Filling the deep, empty place—what some have called the soul—often means finding the truth, giving life value. This is what religion is all about: not only in Unitarian Universalism, but in any religion. The need for meaning is not a physiological or organic need like the need for food and air. Neither is it strictly nor exclusively a psychological need, like the need for nurturance and affirmation. Meaning is a religious need, sustenance for our souls, life for our spirit.

Many suggest that the truth and meaning that people are searching for is God. Yet nowhere in Unitarian Universalism's seven principles is God mentioned. (God is mentioned once in the sources section.) Truth and meaning, but not God. If a stranger heard you say you were searching for truth and meaning, he or she might ask: "You mean God, don't you?" Then, how would you respond?

Some have responded: "God is merely a three letter word, a name given to that which we can't name." G-o-d is just a symbol for what many call religious truth and meaning. For some, that truth and meaning is described in the Hindu story of the ultimate turtle on whom everything rests and who, in turn, rests on nothing: it is a mystery. For others, the truth and meaning that is called G-o-d is a way to acknowledge a staggering and awesome complexity that science seeks to decipher with theories and formulas. The mythologist and folklorist Joseph Campbell describes this truth and meaning as "the universal doctrine."

Briefly formulated, the universal doctrine teaches that all the visible structures of the world—all things and beings—are the effects of a ubiquitous power out of which they rise, which supports and fills them during the period of their manifestation, and back into which they must ultimately dissolve. This is the power known to science as energy, to the Melanesians as *mana*, to the Sioux Indians as *wakonda*, the Hindus as *shakti*, and the Christians as the power of God. Its manifestation in the psyche is called, by the psychoanalysts, libido. And its manifestation in the cosmos is the structure and flux of the universe itself.

What we have learned about people's understanding and belief in G-o-d, might best be summed up in this incident related by Alan Watts ("Western Mythology: Its Dissolution and Transformation"):

In 1928 the British Parliament was called upon to authorize a new prayer book for the Church of England. . . . In the course of the debate somebody got up and said, "Isn't it sort of ridiculous that this secular legislative body should be asked to rule upon the affairs of the Church because, after all, there are many atheists among us?" And another member got up and said, "Oh, I don't think there are any atheists here. We all believe in some sort of a something somewhere."

Having heard stories from small group discussions, counseling, after-sermon responses, letters, impromptu remarks, and more, I too have reached the not-all-that-startling conclusion that "we all believe in some sort of something somewhere." For thousands of years and in the culture where we make our home, this "something somewhere" has been designated with the word G-o-d. There are other names, including truth and meaning, but God is a consistent, timeless one. It's just a word, a symbol representing "some sort of something somewhere."

I used to argue about this God word. Of course, I never "won" any of these arguments, and my arguing never made any difference for me or anyone else. In my well-rehearsed, tolerant, open, liberal way I was actually pretty closed-minded when it came to God until I took several theology seminars at a Methodist seminary six years ago. I questioned liberation theology's dependence on belief in God. One morning, after patiently listening to my opinion, my professor quietly cut me off and remarked: "You could be right. But you see, liberation theology doesn't care whether you like its God. In liberation theology, the tension isn't from theism versus atheism as you and others have tried to make it. The tension is theism versus idolatry. So, let's talk about idolatry."

What I knew about idolatry you could put in a thimble, or so I thought. Now I understand that the important question for liberation theology and the critical question for us to ask is not about the existence of God, but who or what is my God? The issue is not the presence of God, but God's importance. It's not about what God is like, but what we are like given the God we believe in. Which is to say that the name (or nature) of the God we follow, that which we call truth and meaning, is written on our faces. There's no hiding it; it's obvious; it's there for everyone to see.

Some confuse truth and meaning for what the philosopher Mortimer Adler describes as the six parts of life. Truth and meaning is found in leisure, labor, eating, slumbering, playing, or idling. Any of these, it is said, is the truth and meaning in life, at least that is how life is lived. It is one of these, or several, that makes life significant; it is what living is about; it is what makes sense of living. But it is idolatry because every one of these can be removed in an instant, and then what becomes of truth and meaning, what then of God? Each of these elements of living are temporary, in flux, shaped and reshaped by the ongoingness of daily living.

What I'm suggesting isn't so much what God is or what truth and meaning are. Ultimately, this will be unique to each person. Instead, I'm asking: What is it that distinguishes religious truth and meaning from the idolatrous, from other parts of living? What is it that makes truth and meaning ultimately significant? What is it that is religious about truth and meaning, about God? Why is it that we would even bother to search for it?

In May 1841, Unitarian minister Theodore Parker explored these issues and questions in a sermon entitled "The

Permanent and Transient in Christianity." In his address, he asked what was timeless about the Christian religion, as well as what was passing or of temporary value. In 1995, the Unitarian Universalist Ministers Association collected and published essays in a volume entitled *The Permanent and Transient in Liberal Religion*. It was their version of building a bridge from Parker to the twenty-first century. One of the editors said that their hope was to publish a collection highlighting the permanent in Unitarian Universalism—as viewed from the professional ministry. But after reading dozens of submissions, all they could find was the transient—nothing of the eternal!

Parker, like my colleagues, wanted what so many others have wanted: to find in their religion an absolute, the eternal, what he was calling the permanent. In his book *Staying Put: Making a Home in a Restless World*, Scott Russell Saunders describes what has been part of the quest in every age, regardless of the setting:

> According to a theory favored by many physicists, the universe bloomed from the breaking of symmetry in the first smidgen of a second after the Big Bang. . . . When Buddhism speaks about recognizing our true Self, or Taoism about centering ourselves in the Way, or Judaism about Eden before the Fall, or Christianity about being One in Christ, they point, longingly, toward an unbroken symmetry, a primal unity.

The desire for unity, to be at one with the world, to be centered in everything that we make and have our being, this desire for wholeness is a feature of religious truth and meaning that I hear over and over. Adler's six parts of life, if lived as truth and meaning, will stand in the way of wholeness. But into each could be breathed unity. Who hasn't had at some point in their living, even for just an instant, known something of this wholeness, symmetry, or oneness? It's a characterization of the holy, of that word G-o-d or others like it that represent truth and meaning in our lives. It seems that even when we've never felt it, or experienced enough of it, still we yearn for it and we turn to religion for direction and support.

But why? What is there about religion, real or perceived, that is so appealing? Some of it is tradition—people have been turning to religions for a long, long time when seeking clarity. And we can't dismiss all those who say that religion is what set them "right"—television, radio, the print media, even neighbors and family all report that religion is "the way." But in addition to this, I would include dissatisfaction. Religion, in part, is maintained because of dissatisfaction—when what you are doesn't match what you want; when living doesn't feel right in spite of a good job, good relationships, adequate compensation, enough sleep, most of the things you need to be happy: still, something's off.

When everything you always wanted isn't enough—arriving at this realization can be the starting point in religion. It is no easy thing to confront this dissatisfaction. The need to incorporate unity and wholeness into everything that we do and are, to become at one with life by whatever name given this process or realization—be it truth, meaning, or God—is demanding. Beginning this journey is a bold show of courage, a sacred and holy act that may know no end, a journey that has been commonplace for millennia, begun by millions, and given more names than we will ever know.

The choices and decisions are many. I once had a favorite restaurant in a nearby city. The food was OK, but that's not why I took friends and family there: it was the menu! In some restaurants when the waiter comes to take your order, you're not ready because you can't decide what you want after having read all the choices. In this restaurant, you weren't ready the first, second, maybe even the fourth time because you hadn't finished reading the menu! It was great: about twenty pages long, with wonderful illustrations, creative and very funny descriptions of the entrees. Even after you ordered your food, you still wanted to read the menu—often, the menu became the dinner conversation! In other words, you went to this restaurant for the menu! And you brought people there because you couldn't describe it—you had to be there!

Jewish theologian and mystic Martin Buber would have found this restaurant frustrating. He "[defined] religion as experiencing God and theology as talking about God, [explaining] that the difference between religion and theology is the difference between having dinner and reading a menu." With all of my years of reading, studying, and writing, as a minister in the Unitarian Universalist faith tradition, sometimes I feel as though I've been cursed as a reader of menus. Just to experience religion, I tell myself, just to know it would be glorious. Does religion always have to be a search, a journey—must one always be looking without ever finding, arriving, reaching the end? Must I always be reading the menu, never completing the meal?

Unitarian Universalism could be characterized as having a menu approach to truth and meaning. A uniqueness about our search that strikes many who come to Unitarian Universalism—and keeps many of us coming back—is the absence of dogma and creed, the lack of orthodox symbols, the few rituals that appear as necessities on the way to truth and meaning. All of these, a Unitarian Universalist might say, could be explicit and implicit ways of telling a person "Here, just do this and you'll find God." This is a message unlikely to be heard in any Unitarian Universalist setting where the menu of choices often seem limitless, even overwhelming.

"A free and responsible search. . . ." That's it. In *The Structure and Dynamics of the Psyche*, psychologist Carl Jung suggests that the search is the answer: "The serious problems in life are never really solved. If ever they should appear to be so it is a sure sign that something has been lost. The meaning and purpose of a problem seems to be not in its solution, but in our working at it incessantly." As Jung suggests, I too am dubious when people tell me that they have found the truth and meaning—the Answer—and they are no longer on a search, on their journey. I wonder if they have lost their map or their map is outdated! Some get stalled: There are rest stops along the way, oases that easily become distractions instead of opportunities to refresh the soul and refuel the spirit.

Like going to that restaurant, Unitarian Universalism affirms not only a search for truth and meaning, but also that the search is "where it's at," the journey is "what it's

61

all about," to search *is* an answer. Maybe Buber was wrong: Reading the menu is a religious experience. Some won't agree: To them, "religious search" is an oxymoron. They say that the purpose of religion is to find the answer, to bring the search to an end, or at the very least to get pointed toward the end.

What is important about this search, about the Unitarian Universalist journey, is living it. That must sound shallow, but this is what I mean: Jung suggests that the meaning and purpose of life is a problem in need of a solution. His idea of working suggests searching, an ongoing quality to life: you just don't arrive at an end. Where I part company with Jung is his characterization of life's meaning and purpose as a problem. Living is not a problem to be solved. A philosophy with this as its goal will ultimately be a futile one. You don't try to solve life. You live life: Life is not a problem to be solved but a mystery to be lived, a far more interesting and exciting perspective.

Our search is marked by the tension and balance of freedom and responsibility: As we live our search, as we live the mystery of life, we covenant to affirm and promote a way that is both free and responsible. Free because we know that every person is unique—in the first principle we affirm an individual's inherent worth and dignity, and with that comes free will, the freedom to believe as your conscience dictates. It's your search and no one else's. A responsible search because the right of conscience demands it: You're not just "a loose canon" in search of whatever works. In the more orthodox faiths, freedom is checked by the responsibility of authority—whether it be from tradition, the hierarchy, or sacred scripture and liturgy. In Unitarian Universalism, while these may hold value, they are not the final authority; they alone won't balance freedom and responsibility. Balance comes from each person: human experience is the final authority. Lessons are learned from tradition, leadership, and the world's sacred scriptures, as well as from life experiences, but eventually we each provide balance to our search; we give direction to our lives.

What does this direction look like? Consider the lessons you have been exposed to, consider the sources and traditions from which our faith draws. How might we characterize our free and responsible search (for truth and meaning)?

Our search must be characterized by humility. In a free and responsible search, we are aware and humbled by our shortcomings, fears, uncertainties, and contradictions. The lesson of this story from Anthony de Mello's *One Minute Wisdom* speaks of this humility:

To a visitor who described himself as a seeker after Truth, the teacher said: "If what you seek is Truth, there is one thing you must have above all else." "I know," answered the student, "an overwhelming passion for it." "No," said the teacher, "an unremitting readiness to admit you may be wrong."

I like the readings in our hymnal entitled "Confessions" and "Meditations and Prayers," because they help me to focus and get grounded. I know I need confession and reflection, I need to think before I speak, and sometimes I need to speak less and be silent more. Humility in the free and responsible search is essential.

The awareness of oneself and others is also essential. To be honest, authentic, and open is paramount to religious searching and living. Awareness of where your experiences come from and where they are leading; awareness of how others respond to your search; awareness of who and what makes you comfortable and what makes you anxious, and being able to verbalize both; awareness of former religious traditions and what you found affirming and challenging; awareness of motivations, resistance, and tendencies all can be critical to your search.

It is also important that a search be nonjudgmental. The fourth principle doesn't say *the*, but *a* free and responsible search. This implies that there is more than one search. There could be as many searches as there are people. Being nonjudgmental doesn't mean an absence of disagreements: Nonjudgmental means that disagreements don't become personal attacks, insults, or thoughtless stereotypes.

A fourth feature of our search is balance. A piece by David Rankin entitled "Fetish on Fads" speaks of balance:

> I felt sorry for Jake. We were friends in seminary—many years ago. He was now a broken soul.
>
> When he was a college student, he was into existentialism—Camus, Sartre, and Kierkegaard.
>
> When he was a graduate student, he was into world religions—Taoism, Hinduism, and Buddhism.
>
> When he was a theological student, he was into the new psychology—Fromm, Rogers, and Maslow.
>
> When he was a minister, he was into experimental worship—guitars, folk-songs, and dialogue.

When he was a community organizer, he was into direct action—marches, sit-ins, and rallies.

When he was a welfare recipient, he was into human
potential—EST, Rolfing, and holistic medicine.

Jake had discovered all kinds of things—but never the
center of himself. He could not dance in the empty
spaces, or listen to the sound of no birds singing.

The difficulty and hardship for Jake, and others like him,
is never being in one place long enough to enjoy the truth
and meaning that might be there, not staying at an oasis
long enough to fuel the spirit and nurture the soul. For
Jake and others, the search has so many stops and starts,
turns and detours that it's no wonder they can't center
and focus. It's a journey, not a race; a search, not a scav-
enger hunt; for a lifetime, not until the next book comes
out or a fad begins. The see-saw approach is unbalanced
and leads nowhere. The free and responsible search is characterized by balance.

Our search is distinguished by learning. Every new
insight or revelation, each time there's a breakthrough or
an "ah-ha," it is not dismissed but embraced, valued, and
celebrated. Ram Dass remarked that "The spiritual journey is falling on your face and starting over." Our journey is a learning experience instead of a search for the
answer.

A free and responsible search means being engaged with
the world instead of transcending it. Some become frustrated in their searches, frustrated with feeling as though
they are going nowhere. A quick way to resolve this frus-
tration is to abandon this world—to pursue or embrace

another reality that holds the answer. Many religious traditions have a story that speaks about this answer. In *The Heart of the Enlightenment*, Anthony de Mello wrote:

A young man became obsessed with a passion for Truth so he took leave of his family and friends and set out in search of it. He traveled over many lands, sailed across many oceans, climbed many mountains, and all in all, went through a great deal of hardship and suffering.

One day he awoke to find he was seventy-five years old and had still not found the Truth he had been searching for. So he decided, sadly, to give up the search and go back home.

It took him months to return to his hometown for he was an old man now. Once home, he opened the door of his house—and there he found that Truth had been patiently waiting for him all those years.

This story and hundreds like it, remind us that what we search for is often closer than we realize. This doesn't mean that we abandon our search. There is value in the search itself. A free and responsible search engages life not in a distant or transcendent location or reality. It is a search here and now.

A free and responsible search for truth and meaning requires focused attention. Intentionality and deliberateness are crucial: Our search is not a casual thing, not a hobby. When we embrace our searches (or are embraced by it), like a beacon directing us down a path—when our desire for truth and meaning becomes a religious search—

it receives our attention, our focus, because the light of truth and meaning cannot be ignored.

"We covenant to affirm and promote a free and responsible search—a search characterized by humility, awareness, nonjudgment, balance, learning, engagement, and focusing. It is *a* search, not *the* search; it is done per person, one at a time. Yet it is not done alone. "We *covenant* to affirm and promote. . . ." That's not the language of one hand clapping! "*We covenant* . . ." is the language of religious community. Our "free and responsible search," although an individual journey, is done in community. "Thank goodness!" I say. Unitarian Universalist pagan Margot Adler adds: "To be truthful about it, not everything comes from personal experience and revelation. There are times when gut and heart and intuition are not enough [and] it's important to have a reality check, people who will bring us down to earth . . ." The value and role of a congregation—the community of like-minded searchers—is what gives our individual journeys support and context, it gives each one of us reasons to keep our search free and responsible.

There is much to be learned on a journey or, staying with Buber's analogy, a lot can be learned from reading the menu. Reading the menu doesn't guarantee a meal, and being on a free and responsible search doesn't guarantee truth and meaning. But covenanting together, as a congregation and not alone, we can walk the search, sharing what we learn, discovering that while the truth and meaning we seek could be as different and unique as each of us are, our desire for religious wholeness or "atonement"—our dream of peace for our world and peace within ourselves—is a common one. Let us "covenant to affirm and promote a free and responsible search for truth and meaning," and let us celebrate our faith community called Unitarian Universalism.

The Right of Conscience and the Use of the Democratic Process Within Our Congregations and in Society at Large

EARL K. HOLT III

It may seem unusual for a religious body to include a commitment to a political method in its defining principles. Neither the word democracy, nor for that matter the word conscience, appeared in earlier purpose statements of the American Unitarian Association or the Universalist Church of America, the two national bodies that consolidated to form the Unitarian Universalist Association in 1961. Nevertheless, commitments to both individual liberty of conscience and to democratic principles were implicit in both traditions and became more explicit at the time of merger.

The right or freedom of conscience was symbolized on the Universalist side by the so-called "Liberty Clause," which early on was attached to its thrice-recast Declaration of Faith, first adopted in Philadelphia in 1790. Each version of this Universalist Declaration of Faith, creedal in form, enunciated the beliefs of the church as a whole; but the Liberty Clause anticipated and made allowance for a variety of individual interpretations, stating that "neither this nor any other statement shall be imposed as a creedal test, provided that the faith thus indicated be professed." The ambiguity of this language must be acknowledged, but the intent to allow latitude is clear.

Commitment to individual freedom of belief was even more emphatic on the Unitarian side. In part this relates to an essential difference between the two bodies: The Universalists conceived of themselves as a "denomination" in the formal sense; they were organized as a national church. The Unitarians, on the other hand, were organized from the beginning as an "association" of churches, autonomous and independent congregations organized around their own individual covenants, which were less belief statements than statements of corporate purpose. In the language of its bylaws: "The [American Unitarian] Association recognizes that its constituency is congregational in polity and that individual freedom of belief is inherent in the Unitarian tradition. Nothing in these purposes shall be construed as an authoritative test."

Similar language was retained in the UUA Bylaws at the time of the Unitarian Universalist merger, and the two bodies were organized as an association of "autonomous, self-governing local churches and fellowships" along with the further reiteration that, "Nothing in these Bylaws shall be construed as infringing upon the congregational polity or internal self-government of member societies, including the exclusive right to call and ordain its own minister or ministers, and to control its own property and funds." (This was, by the way, a polite but emphatic rejection of the Universalist polity, which was more presbyterial than congregational and under which state conventions commonly held title to church property and had the power to ordain clergy.) In addition, the charter bylaws of the newly merged Association included among its statement of corporate purposes: "To affirm, defend, and promote the supreme worth of every human personality, the dignity of man, and the use of the democratic method in human relationships."

Again, it may seem surprising to find a stated commitment to democratic method or process among the core purposes of a religious organization, but perhaps less so if one remembers that Unitarian Universalism is based on two religions born in the New World in the formative years of the American Republic, each of them decisively influenced and shaped in their formative years by the same Enlightenment ideas and values that gave rise to the American Revolution and American democracy. It is no accident that so many of the founders of the Republic were also leaders in the formation of these American denominations, including, among others, Benjamin Rush, Universalist and signer of the Declaration of Independence, and Joseph Priestley, the scientist and Unitarian preacher who was a strong influence on Thomas Jefferson and John Adams. Their religious convictions were crucial in their formulation of America's political creed, for as James Madison would say later, "What is government itself but the greatest of all reflections on human nature?" Political and religious ideas interpenetrate. For example, the political notion that a people have a right to self-government grows out of a religious conviction that human beings have the capacity to shape their own destiny, that they are not mere puppets on a divine string.

Democracy, to put it another way, is more than a mechanism of governance. It is an expression of faith in the power of human beings to shape their own lives, a faith that is most explicit in the ideals of our religious tradition.

In this century, the most articulate and important advocate of this faith, which he termed "America's Real Religion," was A. Powell Davies, minister of All Souls Unitarian Church in Washington, DC, until his untimely death in 1957. Davies was arguably the most significant Unitarian minister of our era. He seems to have coined the phrase, "the democratic process in human relations" as one of our key principles. Democracy in his view "is the social and political expression of [a] religious principle," that all human beings are kin and humankind a family; "and at this higher level," he said, "the spiritual unity of the human family is declared to be unrestricted by nation, race, or creed." This "Religion of Democracy," as it has been called, or "The Faith Behind Freedom" is obviously not intended to be the unique possession or treasured value of a single sect or denomination, ours or any other. Its application is universal, and so we commit ourselves to its implementation not only among ourselves, within our own congregations, but in society at large as part of a vision of a "world community with peace, liberty, and justice for all."

It is important to note, however, that in the UUA Purposes and Principles, our covenantal commitment to the democratic process is explicitly linked, not to a social goal, but to the protection of an individual right: freedom of conscience. Democracy, as Winston Churchill famously noted, is the worst form of government—except for all the others. All forms of government, being merely human inventions, are flawed; and all, including democracy, are subject to abuse. Without a firm commitment to the right of every individual to freedom of thought and expression, in simplest terms the right to be wrong, democracy itself can degenerate into a tyranny of the majority, as Jefferson warned in his first inaugural address: "All, too, will bear in mind this sacred principle," he said, "that though the will of the majority is in all cases to prevail, that will, to be rightful, must be reasonable; that the minority possess equal rights, which equal laws must protect, and to violate which would be oppression."

In adopting their Liberty Clause the Universalists fundamentally altered the nature of their Declaration of Faith. After all, a creed with a built-in allowance for conscientious objection is no longer quite a creed! The Unitarians never formally adopted any similar statements of faith, and if any single principle can be said to be paramount in the history of American Unitarianism, it would have to be individual freedom of belief. In consequence, both movements have experienced increasing theological diversity over their whole history. Both began as heretical ideologies within historical Protestantism, as dissents from orthodoxy; both evolved, separately and then together, into a movement characterized most notably by wide theological diversity. This was not accomplished without periods of extreme tension, dissent, and struggle, a process that has not ended and presumably never will.

What, then, holds this diversity together? The current purposes and principles represent one answer to that question. Properly understood, and like similar formulations of the past, it is descriptive and not prescriptive, suggestive and not authoritative. It is also destined in time to be replaced by something else; indeed, it has already been amended once since its initial adoption, by a vote taken at a General Assembly, and presumably will be again. Nonetheless, there is an understandable tendency to view such statements as creedal or quasi-creedal; to see them as not just a statement but *the* statement of Unitarian Universalist orthodoxy. Which is why an understanding of the meaning of this fifth principle is so crucial to the whole: "We covenant to affirm . . . the right of conscience and the use of the democratic process within our congregations and in society at large."

In recent years, the most articulate and tireless advocate of this principle within our tradition was the Reverend Paul H. Beattie (1937-1989), founder of the organization Unitarian Universalists for Freedom of Conscience. Following in the spirit of the Unitarian minister William Ellery Channing, Beattie articulated the vision of a church that would encourage the widest possible diversity and pluralism by a radical application of the free mind principle. He was particularly concerned about the modern tendency in our movement toward political formism, but he wanted a church that was inclusi the broadest terms. "I want my Unitarian Universalist church to include Christians, Theists, Humanists, and others," he said, "I want its political discussions to include Republicans, Democrats, Consumerists, and Libertarians. I want its discussions of economics to include Milton Friedmanites and John Kenneth Galbraithians, marxists, socialists and capitalists, or free enterprisers. Such inclusiveness, which grows out of a radical congregational polity, the free mind principle, and the noncreedal approach to religion, is the only possible basis for modern Unitarian Universalism."

What is unique and precious to Unitarian Universalism is that we affirm no external authority in our religious lives, not of church or creed or Bible, but hold as authoritative only the internal voice of conscience that speaks in each and every human soul. And as we grow in knowledge and experience, we come to new and different religious understandings. Our religious lives are works in progress. This is obviously true individually, but it is also true of our religious tradition as a whole. So we are organized both as a church and as an association, as a democracy, because a democracy too is a work in progress. It changes according to the changes desired and expressed by its constituency. Conscience and democracy work together, though sometimes uncertainly and always imperfectly.

A Revolutionary War soldier named Ames described the difference between monarchy and democracy in an analogy to a three-masted sailing ship and a raft. The one is beautiful and impressive on the high seas, he said, but in rough weather can be shattered and sunk against the shoals. The raft of democracy, on the other hand, is virtually unsinkable, he observed, but you always have your feet wet.

Unitarian Universalism is a religion in which, metaphorically speaking, you always have your feet wet. And so there is always a temptation in and among us, to seek to establish something more like the sailing ship, something apparently more safe and more certain. In a prophetic sermon entitled "The Only Basis for Unitarian Universalism," Paul Beattie called this temptation the great illusion, and it deserves to be quoted at length:

> The survival of our religious movement or any like it will always be in doubt, not from without but within, for in each age large numbers of people will be anxious and ready to abandon this approach to religion for something which seems to promise greater certainty, greater assurance. We have to learn and relearn in each generation that the quest for certainty is the great illusion. We have to learn and relearn in each generation how wonderful it is to say to each person who comes to us: in religion—in life—you must learn to think for yourself and act for yourself—no one can or should do it for you. Many, many people hunger to hear this message and to live it. There is no substitute for the freedom of the mind and the heart and the conscience which I am describing. If we allow it, we shall fulfill our great and unique potential in religion. If we do not, the people I am describing will leave our ranks and their

kind will cease to be drawn to our way in religion. Our churches are voluntary associations. No one has to join us. It is not at all certain that the free way in religion . . . will survive to the end of the human experiment on this planet—but the people whom I most admire—and with whom I will always cast my lot—are those who deeply cherish and want to live in the free religious community . . . and for them, nothing else will satisfy.

It is the elevation of individual conscience to the primary category of religious authority that has been the uniquely distinguishing characteristic of liberal religious theology from Channing's time to our own. The purpose of life from this perspective is the opportunity it presents to grow a soul, to gradually unfold the moral and religious forces within us, employing all the resources at our disposal. We believe that the individual conscience is the only legitimate source of religious authority and that the purpose of the church is to grow and nurture individual conscience. There are no limits to the growth of this moral and religious force within us, if we will nourish it faithfully.

The Goal of World Community With Peace, Liberty, and Justice for All

JOHN BUEHRENS

At the time of the bicentennial of American independence in 1976, the distinguished historian Henry Steele Commager, a Unitarian Universalist, drafted a "Declaration of Interdependence." Its preamble began:

> When in the course of history the threat of extinction confronts humankind, it is necessary for the people of this nation to declare their interdependence with the people of all nations and to embrace those principles and build those institutions which will enable us to survive and civilization to flourish. . . .
>
> We hold these truths to be self-evident: that all

people are created equal; that the inequalities and injustices which afflict so much of the human race are the product of history and society, not of God or nature; that people everywhere are entitled to the blessings of life and liberty, peace and security and the realization of their full potential; that they have an inescapable moral obligation to preserve those rights for posterity; and that to achieve these ends all the peoples and nations of the globe should acknowledge their interdependence . . . and acknowledge that the forces that unite us are incomparably deeper than those that divide us—that all people are part of one global community, dependent upon one body of resources, bound together by the ties of a common humanity and associated in a common adventure on the planet Earth.

Just as the drafters and signers of the original Declaration of Independence included many early Unitarians (John Adams, Thomas Jefferson) and Universalists (Dr. Benjamin Rush), twentieth-century work on behalf of the United Nations and other efforts toward a world community with peace, liberty, and justice has had strong Unitarian Universalist support.

Only twice has a UUA General Assembly gone beyond passing a simple resolution and promulgated a so-called "consensus statement." One was on racial equality and justice, passed in 1966. The second was a "Statement of Consensus on the United Nations," passed in June 1969.

From the beginning of the Association's existence there has been a Unitarian Universalist United Nations

Office. Along with the Unitarian Universalist Women's Federation and the Unitarian Universalist Service Committee, the UU-UNO is one of only three continent-wide "Associate Member Organizations" of the UUA. It has broad voluntary membership, a network of "UN envoys," funding from special UN Sunday collections, and programs that both represent us among Non-Governmental Organizations (NGO) at the United Nations and help to keep us informed. Unitarian Universalists have chaired important NGO committees at the United Nations—on disarmament, religious liberty, and other justice issues.

This is not just secular, political work, but profoundly religious. The late Jewish sage Martin Buber once addressed a United Nations conference in Rome. There he told a parable about the modern world.

At the beginning of the modern world, at the time of the American and French revolutions, three ideals were said to walk hand in hand: liberty, equality, and what was then called "fraternity." Today we might call the last, more inclusively, the spirit of kinship.

In the course of revolutionary upheaval, however, the ideals separated. Liberty went West, to America first of all. But it changed its character along the way. It became confused with mere freedom from restraint, freedom to exploit the land and exploit others. Equality did not extend to Native Americans, African slaves, and women.

Meanwhile Equality went East. Through more revolutions in Russia and China, however, it too changed character, and not for the better. It became the equality of the *gulag*, of millions of people all waving the same "Little Red Book."

The third element went into hiding. Kinship, the sense that we are all sisters and brothers together, children of one great Mystery, was the linking ideal, the religious principle. Yet modern intellectuals and revolutionaries scorned religion, so this ideal took to hiding among communities of the powerless, where a sense of connectedness and kinship, stronger than Western individualism, deeper than Eastern collectivism, survived.

From there this religious spirit has gradually emerged again. Early in the twentieth century, many people thought that religion would simply wither away. It has reappeared, however, in every powerful attempt to reunite the separated: in efforts like those of Dr. Martin Luther King, Jr., here in the West, to reunite to our vaunted liberties some equality, at least of opportunity; in Poland's Solidarity movement, which began the effort to restore to socialist equality some degree of spiritual liberty.

Which brings me to Tienanmen Square in China, where the Statue of Liberty was raised in 1990, only to be suppressed again. Buber insisted that the ideals behind the modern experiment cannot be fulfilled without the reemergence, in nonexclusive forms, of the religious spirit of kinship.

Not long ago, I visited China as one of the leaders of the World Conference on Religion and Peace (WCRP), founded by my predecessor, Dr. Dana McLean Greeley, just as he finished serving as the first president of the UUA (1961-1969). The WCRP is now the world's strongest international, interfaith organization. Its first secretary general was Greeley's close associate, Unitarian Universalist minister Dr. Homer Jack.

A generation ago in China, the Communist Party tried violently to suppress all religion. During the so-called "Cultural Revolution," every shrine, temple, mosque, monastery, church, and seminary in China was closed. Religious leaders were sent to forced labor. Training stopped, so that those that I met in 1996 were either nearing eighty years old or barely thirty. Along with the current secretary general of WCRP, I met with the top leaders of China's five main religious groups, Buddhist, Protestant, Catholic, Muslim, and Taoist.

At a banquet given for us in the Great Hall of the People, we spoke of religion as the element in every culture that preserves the deepest memories and wisdom of humankind and supports a sense of kinship. I presented the Communist officials who oversee religion with symbolic gifts from Monticello: small pewter cups and simple wooden pen-trays, both designed by Thomas Jefferson, author of the Virginia Statute for Religious Freedom, the world's first such democratic legislation protecting religious freedom.

Today only about fifteen percent of China's huge population has any sort of religious identity at all. Yet even intellectuals are beginning to reassess religion. All that remains of Marxism, one remarked, is the materialism. The moral and spiritual vacuum is huge. The liberalized economy is expanding at a rapid rate. Consumer spending had grown twenty-five percent in one year. Crime, likewise. The gap between rich and poor, perhaps even faster. Shortly after our visit, the Communist Party recruited religious leaders to help them promulgate what is surely one of the most astonishing slogans ever chosen by a nominally Marxist regime: "Renounce Scientific Materialism; Embrace Spiritual Civilization!"

One can't read such phrases without being stunned by the irony. Yet surely "civilization," like "community," *does* depend upon spiritual, relational qualities.

"A better global order cannot be created or enforced by laws alone. . . . Both the minds and hearts of women and men must be addressed. . . . Earth cannot be changed for the better unless the consciousness of individuals is changed also." These words come from a document called *Towards a Global Ethic*, developed in a broad interfaith dialogue led by theologian Hans Kung and promulgated following the 1993 Centennial Parliament of the World's Religions, held in Chicago. (The first Parliament of the World's Religions, held at the Chicago World's Fair of 1893, had as its organizing secretary a Unitarian minister, the Reverend Jenkin Lloyd Jones.)

The signers included representatives of nearly every religious tradition on planet Earth. "By a global ethic," they declared, "we do not mean a global ideology or a single unified religion beyond all existing religions, and certainly not the domination of one religion over all others. By a global ethic we mean a fundamental consensus on binding values."

"No one has the right to use her or his possessions without concern for the needs of society and Earth," declares *Towards a Global Ethic*. Deep and unresolved differences concerning cultural norms about family life and sexuality are acknowledged, but a world-wide "culture of equal rights and partnership between women and men" is urged. Principles for addressing questions of environmental and economic justice are suggested. Above all, the use of religious and ethnic differences to foster hatred and violence is condemned, on the basis of the best wisdom of all the world's faiths.

"Every act of violence committed in the name of God is an act of violence against God," declared Bartolomeos, the Ecumenical Patriarch of Constantinople and leader of the world's Christian Orthodox communities, in addressing the Orthodox Church of Serbia during the Bosnian crisis of the mid-1990s. "Violence in the name of faith is inherently faithless." Like the Vatican, the World Council of Churches, the Muslim World League, and many others, the Patriarch supports a project of long-term, grassroots efforts at reconciliation in Bosnia. Political manipulation, playing on religious and ethnic differences, lies behind many conflicts that seem outwardly to be about religion.

Most so-called "religious wars" aren't really about religion at all. They're about power. When religion goes away, questions about who has power and how it is used don't vanish. In fact, they can become more difficult than ever. For as Dr. King once said clearly, "One of the great problems of history is that the concepts of love and power have usually been contrasted as opposites—polar opposites—so that love is identified with a resignation of power, and power with a denial of love. . . . What is needed is a realization that power without love is reckless and abusive, and love without power is sentimental and anemic. Power at its best is love implementing the demands of justice, and justice at its best is power correcting everything that stands against love."

Several years ago I was in Ahmedabad, India, where Gandhi once had his ashram. I was at a conference center meeting with the leaders of nearly two dozen social change programs, mostly aimed at the empowerment of women, especially among the poorest of the poor. At the close of the evening, the group began to sing what they called "struggle songs."

One was sung in English, then in Hindi, Gujarati, Tamil, Bengali, Punjabi, Maharashtri, and other languages represented there. It was "We Shall Overcome."

At first I didn't really know why I felt so overcome, why tears were streaking my cheeks. Perhaps it was because I knew the song's origins. The tune came from Africa. It became a hymn among the Gullah people of the Georgia Sea Islands, who still speak an African dialect. The words said, "I shall overcome." From there it was taken by a Unitarian Universalist named Guy Carawan to a conference in East Tennessee. One night, he and Zilphia Horton penned the words that made the song say, "we." What I was hearing was a yearning for kinship, carried by slaves from one continent to another, lifted up by people I knew, now being carried into the struggles of poor women half a world away and into their dialects. Suddenly the whole concept of "world community" became more than a goal for me. It became something real, not merely a possibility, but an overwhelming imperative.

Those women in India also showed me that if one thing is needed for the sense of human kinship to be restored, it is not declarations, ethics, or even songs. It is the full empowerment of the world's women.

Begun in the early 1980s with some unsolicited trust money that came to the UUA for "the benefit of the people of India," the Unitarian Universalist Holdeen India Program helps to demonstrate that truth. It works with grassroots groups that empower women—like the Self-Employed Women's Association (SEWA). As industrialization has drawn men away from the villages and into the cities and industrial areas, SEWA has organized over 100,000 women just in the province of Gujarat alone. They form agricultural cooperatives, redeem damaged land, sell crafts together, do micro-banking, and develop skills ranging from drip-irrigation to video and computers. In urban slums, Hindu and Muslim women are supported by the Holdeen India Program in organizing clinics and programs against communal violence. It is not mere social development. Because human rights are emphasized and advocacy skills supported and encouraged, it's real empowerment, in which the goal of community becomes more real, first locally, then globally.

At the 1995 United Nations World Conference on Women, held in Beijing, China, women from SEWA and other Holdeen partner groups met with women from Haiti, Eritrea, Zaire, and elsewhere, sponsored by the Unitarian Universalist Service Committee—not to mention over a hundred Unitarian Universalist women from North America who were present.

The Unitarian Universalist Service Committee (UUSC), founded in 1939 to assist refugees from Nazism, has become perhaps the single most important organization through which Unitarian Universalists work for "the world community with peace, liberty, and justice for all."

Supported by tens of thousands of voluntary member-contributors, the UUSC works to advance justice and human rights both in the United States and abroad. Its current domestic emphasis is called "Promise the Children," and focuses on the human rights of American children in poverty. It develops curricula like *Gender Justice: Women's Rights Are Human Rights*. Overseas, its projects focus not only on women's issues, but also on democratization and refugees. In Canada, there is a parallel Unitarian Service Committee that does such exemplary work that it receives Canadian governmental support.

Like most religious groups, the Unitarian Universalist Association in North America has affiliates abroad with which it maintains a special sense of global kinship through the International Council of Unitarians and Universalists. Some of the member groups have been in existence for centuries.

There are roughly 100,000 Hungarian-speaking Unitarians in Hungary and in the Transylvania region of Romania. Their origins go back to the 1500s. In the midst of the great religious conflicts that followed the Reformation, their founder, Francis Dávid, declared that "we need not think alike to love alike." Although more traditional in worship and theology than our North American Unitarian Universalist congregations (they elect Unitarian bishops, for example!), the Unitarian churches and villages of Transylvania and Hungary have been tremendously aided, especially since the Romanian Revolution of 1989, through "partner church" relationships with congregations in North America and Great Britain. There are over two hundred Unitarian congregations in Britain, most of them small but very historic, with another thirty-five or so "non-subscribing Presbyterian" congregations in Northern Ireland, who are unitarian in theology, if not in name.

In the mid-nineteenth century, in the Khasi Hills of Northeast India, Calvinists from Wales converted the area's tribal people—who are not ethnically related to most Indians, but more to the Khmers of Cambodia. After a time, one of the more thoughtful converts, Harom Kissor Singh, approached the missionaries. I like to imagine him saying this:

"Thank you for introducing us to the wonderful spiritual and moral teachings of Jesus. Very profound. Only one small question: Why do you ask us to believe so many things *about* him? Wasn't Jesus simply a human being, who taught that we are all children of one God? That we should show this by treating one another always as sisters and brothers? The one God he called Father, our tribal religion, before you came, called Mother, and must be the same God the Muslims call Allah and that the Hindus have so many names for, no?"

"No!" said the missionaries. "We know your kind back in Wales: you're a Unitarian!"

"Thank you for that, too," said Singh. "It is always good to know one is not alone in the world. May I have that address?" He founded a church with help from British Unitarians. A Unitarian prayer book and hymns were developed in Khasi. Schools sponsored by each congregation were offered as an alternative to the mission schools, and greatly developed during the thirty-year residence among the Khasis of Margaret Barr, a British Unitarian. Today there are over thirty-five congregations and schools, with over 10,000 Khasi Unitarians.

There are some scattered offshoots of British Unitarianism in places like South Africa, Australia, and New Zealand. There are small indigenous congregations in Lagos, Nigeria, and Madras, South India. There is a seventeen-congregation Unitarian Universalist Church of the Philippines. More recently new Unitarian Universalist groups have developed, quite spontaneously, in Sri Lanka, Pakistan, Russia, Latvia, Poland, and elsewhere. The International Council of Unitarians and Universalists also includes a lay-led German group and a network called the European Unitarian Universalist Community.

Almost all of these groups are, in turn, part of a larger interfaith organization called the International Association for Religious Freedom (IARF). Originally founded in 1900 as a network of Unitarian and other liberal Christian groups in Europe and America, the IARF is now truly global and interfaith. It includes liberal groups in each of the world's major religious traditions. These include the six million Japanese members of Rissho Kosei Kai, a lay Buddhist organization, and the three million Won Buddhists of Korea, as well as Reconstructionist Judaism, and liberal groups in Islam, Hinduism, and Eastern Orthodoxy.

Work for "the goal of world community with peace, liberty, and justice for all" can't be done effectively by any one religious group alone. Unitarian Universalists are proud to have been pioneers in realizing that truth, and in building structures for international, interfaith cooperation.

Respect for the Interdependent Web of All Existence of Which We Are a Part

BARBARA MERRITT

The interdependent web of life is not simply a poetic metaphor. The interdependent web is a fact of our exist-ence; it is an essential way of understanding the world in the twentieth century. The reality of this web has been directly observed by the eye and the senses throughout human history. But we also now know that the interde-pendent web is at work at the subatomic level. Consider Bell's Theorem in Quantum Physics. Take two paired photons, one charged positive, one negative. Alter the polarization of one from negative to positive, and instan-taneously the other photon changes *its* charge. Separate the two photons with 8,000 miles, and six feet of lead, and, again, the moment that one charge is changed, its bonded pair responds in kind. The connection between the paired particles is so profound, that the change occurs no matter what the distance, or the obstacles that seemingly separate them. Put them far enough apart, and the change occurs faster than the speed of light. As physicist Brian Hines writes, "nothing material links the two photons. The connection cannot be shielded by any type of matter or energy, and the strength of their linkage does not diminish with distance" (*God's Whisper, Creations Thunder: Echoes of Ultimate Reality in the New Physics*). This extraordinary connection between two particles in the subatomic level offers a glimpse at just how interconnected our existence really is.

New discoveries in the biological sciences reveal equally remarkable relationships. Giraffes in sub-Saharan Africa are especially fond of eating the leaves of the Massasa tree. As long as not too many of the leaves on a particular tree are consumed, the tree and the giraffe cohabit harmoniously. But when a hungry giraffe consumes so many of the leaves that the tree's well-being is threatened, the tree raises the acidic content in its leaves. The giraffes no longer find them tasteful and stop eating them. Even more remarkable, if there is a wind, then other trees downwind of the Massasa tree raise the levels of acid in *their* leaves, thus sending the giraffes on to another grove of trees to graze. Ecologists are finding that the relationships in any particular ecosystem are complex and pervasive. Every species of plant and animal has a part to play in the health of the whole.

Few, if any, fields of academic study in the twentieth century are not aware of the importance of connections and context. Family therapists know how dramatically a family system affects the outlook and behavior of individuals. Economists acknowledge the impact of a global economy. Historians increasingly include in their study not only events and prominent leaders, but also the cultural forces, the silent participants, and the multidimensional forces that have affected the course of human activity.

When the secular sciences and disciplines clearly recognize the "interdependent web of all existence," what does it mean for Unitarian Universalists to declare it to be one of the principles of our religious faith? It should be obvious to everyone that we are all part of the interdependent web. But what does this interconnection say about the conduct of our life, or the aspirations of the human spirit?

Regretfully, Unitarian Universalists are all too familiar with what existence looks and feels like when we believe or act as though our lives were *not* a part of a larger creation. The human experience of feeling isolated, alienated, and separate from others is a common one. Our own liberal faith puts a strong emphasis on freedom and independence; too often we neglect our need to belong, our contingency, our natural dependence on one another.

Sometimes our liberal faith can become a shelter for our individual arrogance and can hide a subtle disrespect for community. Promoting our independence and individuality, we often ignore the enormous influence of our natural environment. We try to ignore the pain of our neighbors. We dismiss the influence of the larger culture. When we tell ourselves that we are self-made, or that we march to the tune of our own drummer, we adopt the myth that it is possible to live apart. Too often we can advocate a "gated-community of the mind," a life stance in which, under the guise of intellectual discernment, we mark out an exclusive territory. We stockpile our resources, guard our privacy, and reject the experiences and the dignity of those with whom we disagree. In this unconnected place, very dangerous qualities of judgment, self-righteousness, and prejudice thrive.

We Unitarian Universalists put ourselves at risk, not only when we push away other human beings, but also when we reject some fundamental parts of ourselves. In the natural world, some will appreciate and celebrate a harmony, a splendor, a compelling blessing. But they do not include their own existence in this larger reality, because they think of themselves as "the great exception." They will give praise and honor to the oceans and the animals and to their neighbors, but they will not consider themselves worthy, significant, or essential. Such individuals say, "You may be part of the grand design, but because of my family of origin, or my fragile temperament, or my ethnic heritage, or my sexual preference, or my terrible tragedies, or my physical limitations, or my dramatic mood swings, or the place I grew up, or the schools I attended, or *whatever,* I am the great exception." We don't usually announce this publicly, or print it on our stationery, but it is one of the most insidious ways that we separate ourselves from others, the community, reality, and the holy.

Sometimes, by focusing intently on our personal, unique circumstances and convictions, those of us in the liberal faith actively promote a self-differentiation so extreme that we forget all the immensely important values human beings do have in common. Just because we have a multiplicity of experiences about truth, God, and reality, this diversity does not necessarily mean that we don't fundamentally experience life in similar ways. It is normal to stake out one's own territory. Nevertheless, we need to at least look up from our own walled fortresses and ask, "In what ways do I participate in the universal life struggle of which I am a part?"

Which brings us to the seventh principle of the Unitarian Universalist Association. On closer examination it is not just a self-evident proposition about the space we occupy in the world. It is a religious statement that necessitates certain fundamental spiritual truths and disciplines.

The first of these is humility. If we are part of something larger than ourselves, then the arrogance that we are self-made and self-sufficient must end. We must leave behind our delusion that we have control, our imaginative belief that we are safer when we are alone, and our congenital preference for self-centered assessments. We need to open our eyes to our interdependence. In humility, can we accept that we are being pulled and pushed? Can we invite help, grace, and mercy? Can we confess that we do not wish to live stubbornly alone, lost in selfishness? Together we can seek to be strong in ways that open our hearts and our eyes. We can discover the friends, companions, and assistance that accompanies us on each step of our path.

Another spiritual discipline inherent in the seventh principle is a vastly increased compassion, the cognizance and recognition of all existence. When we open our eyes to the interdependent web of existence we get an awful lot of reality, not just the opening rose or the voice of the turtle dove. In the web we find the retroviruses that cripple and kill, and Alzheimer's, and the ultimate death of everyone we love, and tornadoes, and stock market crashes, and relatives we are not fond of, and wars. This interdependent web is certainly not just a romantic tapestry of nature at its most beautiful and inspiring. There is no question that nature can, at times, comfort, soothe, and inspire us. For some people it is the most reliable setting in which they can sense the transcendent, the holy, and the presence of God. But Rabbi Abraham Heschel warns us against worshiping the natural world. In *God in Search of Man* he wrote, "Nature herself is in need of salvation. Pitiless is the silence of the skies. Nature is deaf to our cries and indifferent to our values. Her laws know no mercy or forbearance. They are inexorable, implacable, ruthless. . . . Nature has no heart, no moral life."

The web of existence in which we breathe, move, and have our being includes the often violent struggles for domination and survival, as well as breathtaking sunsets and the smile of a newborn baby. This web of existence is good and evil, comforting and terrible, a web of life, and a web of death. The seventh principle asks us to have a clear and affirming relationship with what is real. We must learn the spiritual discipline of living with respect; respectfully entering into relationship with the many conditions and challenges of this world.

To have respect for all life does not mean that we understand all that goes on in this creation. It certainly does not mean that we approve of all behavior. Surely the interdependent web will break our hearts, as well as restore our souls. To have respect for life itself, for *all* of existence is to recognize a relationship, a covenant, a connection. To attempt to be respectful is fundamentally a faith stance. The word respect comes from the root "to look back," to regard. In this faithful commitment we promise to pay attention. We offer our acknowledgment of reality. Oftentimes what begins as simply a respectful regard for what is true and real can expand into gratitude and reverence for what is true and real.

The spiritual discipline of offering our respectful attention to the interdependent web of life will automatically lead those who wish to advance the seventh principle into the most fundamental of religious practices; acknowledging the consequences of our actions and choices. José Ortega y Gasset stated the connection clearly in *The Viking Book of Aphorism*: Tell me to what you pay attention, and I will tell you who you are. What we choose to pay attention to determines to a large extent what we become. We are not only a part of the grand design of natural selection and evolution; by the decisions we make, by the way we take care of, ignore, or increase the brokenness of our world, we ourselves are profoundly changed.

Seemingly inconsequential human actions, like throwing a cigarette butt or a candy wrapper on the grass, can alter the beauty and well-being of a landscape. But such small, thoughtless acts also damage the perpetrators. In the Hebrew scripture the proverb is simply stated, "Whoever digs a pit will fall into it, and a stone will come back on the one who starts it rolling" [Proverbs 26:27]. Jesus repeated the same truth when he stated, "The measure by which you give is the measure by which you will receive."

[Matthew 7:2]. You can look at the holy scriptures of any of the world religions and find this principle; call it cause and effect, or karma, or compensation. We cannot harm the earth without harming ourselves. We cannot do violence to our own life, or to the lives of others, without that violence eventually having its effect on us. Our own Unitarian minister and essayist, Ralph Waldo Emerson, in his essay entitled "Compensation," puts it bluntly, "The thief steals from himself. The swindler swindles himself."

If we put poisons into the natural environment, we will eventually find that our own water and air is contaminated. On the other hand, if we plant trees and flowers, and protect open green spaces, the resulting beauty will bless not only the whole world, but will also bless those who do the gardening. When we are a part of healing the earth, we will find ourselves being healed. When we damage the environment, we and our children will bear the consequences.

As Unitarian Universalists, we have clearly stated our commitment to do what we can to repair, restore, and promote the web of life. This commitment necessitates the development of our humility, compassion, respect, and a heightened awareness of the consequences of our actions. Yet all of these fine principles are ultimately meaningless if they do not show up in our daily life, if they are not incarnate in our ordinary actions. The cost of affirming our relationship with all of existence is high and demanding. We must sacrifice our self-centeredness if we want to give our attention to a creation that is much larger than our own individuality. This immense sacred relationship in which we find ourselves requires a lifetime of labor.

Indeed, a lifetime of effort is hardly sufficient if we wish to learn to live in harmony with all living beings. This relationship requires our hands-on involvement. Ideally, one should be able to tell simply by watching a Unitarian Universalist's daily behavior, whether or not this seventh principle has any relevance or meaning.

- How do we greet the stranger in our midst? If every soul is a part of the human family, if everyone is a child of God, then it safely can be assumed that we will welcome them with respect and dignity.

- Are we kind and compassionate to other living creatures? A reverence for life, a commitment to live as nonviolently as possible, leads us into life-giving relationships.

- Do we attempt to promote and affirm the well-being of others, especially those who have fewer resources than we do? Those who are prosperous and strong have a moral obligation to work on behalf of life that is at greater risk; whether that life is an endangered species, or a neighbor in need.

- Are we aware and careful of our own impact on the natural environment? Environmentalists tell us that when we throw something away it always shows up somewhere on earth; there is no place that we can call "away." Luxurious high-consumption Western lifestyles are often produced at the expense of world resources, especially those of the developing world.

- Do we actively seek new ways to reestablish our connections with those people we might have previously dismissed, belittled, or disparaged? Even our enemy occupies a place in the interdependent web.

- Do we work not just the soil in our gardens, but also the ground of our hearts; paying attention to those circumstances which break us open, that call us to go deeper, that challenge us to be more responsive to our fellow men and fellow women? Living in "right-relationship," acknowledging our common humanity, will make us more compassionate, more empathetic, and more fully committed to protecting the interests of all generations; especially those yet to come.

The Unitarian novelist Herman Melville wrote, "We cannot live only for ourselves. A thousand fibers connect us. . . . And among those fibers, as sympathetic threads, our actions run as causes, and they come back to us as effects. On a daily basis, we affect the web of all existence, just as we are affected by it."

To acknowledge the interdependent web of all existence is to admit that we live in the midst of mystery. We are supported and sustained by life forces we do not fully understand. We are acting upon others. We are affecting the quality of other lives in everything we do. Every one of us is a part of a much larger story than we can comprehend from our own limited perspective.

Rumi, a thirteenth-century Persian poet, wrote that the reality and the truth we seek are not far away. They are not found after death. They are not locked away in the secret incantations and rituals of priests and temples. They are not a gift reserved for the very wise or for the very good. The reality and truth we seek are close by. We are surrounded by a miraculous energy. We are a part of it.

Common Beliefs

If the trumpet gives an uncertain
sound, who will arm for battle?
—I Corinthians 14:8

After the new Unitarian Universalist Association Principles
and Purposes were adopted in 1985, Denise Davidoff said,
"Now we must begin the work of putting the new purposes and principles into practice, and we must start in
our own Sunday morning worship in our home churches
and societies." Unitarian Universalist congregations did
just that. A visitor to most churches and fellowships will
find framed copies of the principles and purposes displayed
prominently in the building. The principles are used
widely in Sunday services as a unison or responsive reading. The hymnal, *Singing the Living Tradition*, includes a
responsive reading written by Scott Alexander that incor-
porates the principles. In the congregation I serve, we fre-
quently print the principles on the cover of our Order of
Service. Our congregation recites them together in our
new-member joining ceremony. The principles and purposes have become part of the life, work, and worship of
the congregations of the Association (not to mention the

fact that they are part of the bylaws of the Unitarian Universalist Association).

Not everyone, however, is happy with how the principles are being used. Some people are particularly concerned that what Unitarians and Universalists feared through the centuries has become reality: We have adopted a creed.

Have Unitarian Universalists, at long last, enacted a creed? Recall that in my introduction I offered two definitions of creed. The first by the historian Philip Schaff states, "A creed, or rule of Faith, or Symbol, is a confession of faith for public use, or a form of words setting forth with authority certain articles of belief, which are regarded by the framers as being necessary for salvation, or at least for the well-being of the Christian Church." And the second, a narrower interpretation, by historian Robert Hemstreet, defines a creed as "a definitive statement of a church doctrine to which one must subscribe to be a full member of a particular church."

According to Schaff's definition, the UUA Principles and Purposes certainly are set forth for public use. I suppose it could be said that they are set forth with a certain authority; after all, they are an integral part of the bylaws of the Association to which the congregations belong that recite, print, and frame them. I doubt, however, that any Unitarian Universalist would insist that the UUA Principles and Purposes are necessary for salvation. They are not even *necessary* for the well-being of the church, though many would argue that they are *good* for the well-being of the church. According to the stipulations of Schaff's definition, then, the UUA Principles and Purposes could be called a creed, or at least creedal in tone and use.

But what of the Hemstreet definition? I know of no Unitarian Universalist who would consider the UUA Principles and Purposes to be a definitive statement of Unitarian Universalist doctrine, and I know of no congregation in which assent to them is required for membership. Here in Atlanta, we urge people to join us in a public ceremony in which the UUA Principles and Purposes are recited, but we make clear that this is an option. Anyone can become a member of our congregation and, as far as I know, of any Unitarian Universalist congregation, without reciting, let alone affirming, the UUA Principles and Purposes.

One might say, "Well of course. That's not the point. The point is that the UUA Principles and Purposes are being used *as if* they were a creed."

In Hemstreet's terms, at least, there can be no "as if." Either the UUA Principles and Purposes are being used as a definitive statement of doctrine and as a test for membership, or they are not. To the best of my knowledge, they are not. Certainly, however, they are being used in many, if not most, of our congregations in public worship, and they are being used with the conviction that their use is good for the congregation. They are also being used in the belief that their use is good for Unitarian Universalism—that it is good to publicly affirm a statement of beliefs. A minister once told me about a member who walked up to him after a service, pointed to the principles and purposes on the wall, and said, "I read that poster when I first came here. It is what I believe. I knew I was home." No one suggested to this person that he *must* believe in the UUA Principles and Purposes, and no one suggested that they were all there was to believe. It was simply enough to reveal to him that he was in the right place.

I'll not quibble over words in this instance. To "affirm" and to "believe" are surely close enough in meaning as to be synonymous. When we say, "We gather to affirm and promote the inherent worth and dignity of every person," we are confessing, by the use of the term "affirm," that we *believe* that every person is inherently of worth and dignity. We are clearly making a statement of affirmations/beliefs in our principles that is a statement of faith. If it is not *the* creed, it is surely *a* creed of those Unitarian Universalists who speak it. It is not, however, a creed in the sense that assent is required, either for congregations to belong to the Association or for individuals to belong to the congregations.

Another criticism of the UUA Principles and Purposes as they are used in our congregations is that they oversimplify the breadth and complexity of Unitarian Universalist faith and practice. We are far too diverse, it is said, to be summed up by any statement. And, furthermore, some insist, we value individual experience and thought too much to allow any group, any unison reading, to speak for us.

My response to these concerns is that the UUA Principles and Purposes are not an expression of most of what Unitarian Universalists believe. They are only the least of what we believe. Given the religious freedom we grant each other, our ideas, beliefs, and intuitions may range far beyond these affirmations. They may span the universe of ideas now and forevermore. Why should that freedom of belief, that individual right of flight of thought and fancy, discourage us from joining with others in saying *something* of what we commonly affirm?

As the Christian scripture says, "If the trumpet gives an uncertain sound, who will arm for the battle?" I believe that Unitarian Universalists have a religious, moral, and ethical perspective in our era that is vital and crucial. I believe that there *is* a Unitarian Universal*ism*, a conviction, a faith, an ideology. To be silent on everything, out of fear of breaking the creed of not speaking for everyone, leaves us silent in a time when we need to be heard. The message of universal salvation—the message of the inherent worth and dignity of every person—is as much needed in our time as it was in the time of John Murray, one of the founders of Universalism in America.

The UUA Principles and Purposes are not and were never intended to be our final word or the "Here It Is!" sign at the end of a search. What they are is a statement of things commonly believed among us: not a definitive statement, not a final statement, and not a statement that must be accepted to be counted among us. As some have aptly described them, our principles are not the end of the search, they are the map for the search, a guide along the way.

In *Art and Religion*, the Reverend Van Ogden Vogt, who devoted his life to the public expression of Unitarian Universalist faith, wrote many years ago:

There is unquestionably very great good to be derived from the attempt to state as definitely and clearly as possible from time to time the central matters of one's belief. And if anyone objects strenuously to this, they may always write down as the last clause of their creed their belief that all these statements will some day be changed for the better.

—EAF

Bylaws of the Unitarian Universalist Association, 1961-1984

ARTICLE II • PURPOSES

Section C-2-1. Purposes

The Unitarian Universalist Association is empowered to and shall devote its resources to and exercise its corporate powers for religious, educational, and charitable purposes.

Section C-2-2. Principles

1. The Association, dedicated to the prin-
2. ciples of a free faith shall:
3. (a) Support the free and disciplined
4. search for truth as the foundation of
5. religious fellowship;
6. (b) Cherish and spread the universal
7. truths taught by the great prophets
8. and teachers of humanity in every
9. age and tradition, immemorially
10. summarized in the Judeo-Christian
11. heritage as love to God and love to
12. humankind;
13. (c) Affirm, defend, and promote the su-
14. preme worth and dignity of every

15. human personality, and the use of
16. the democratic method in human
17. relationships;
18. (d) Implement the vision of one world
19. by striving for a world community
20. founded on ideals of brotherhood,
21. justice, and peace;
22. (e) serve the needs of member societies;
23. (f) organize new churches and fellow-
24. ships and otherwise extend and
25. strengthen liberal religion;
26. (g) Encourage cooperation among peo-
27. ple of good will in every land.

The Women and Religion Resolution

ADOPTED BY THE GENERAL ASSEMBLY OF THE UNITARIAN UNIVERSALIST ASSOCIATION, JUNE 1977

WHEREAS, a principle of the Unitarian Universalist Association is to "affirm, defend, and promote the supreme worth and dignity of every human personality, and the use of the democratic method in human relationships"; and

WHEREAS, great strides have been taken to affirm this principle within our denomination; and

WHEREAS, some models of human relationships arising from religious myths, historical materials, and other teachings still create and perpetuate attitudes that cause women everywhere to be overlooked and undervalued; and

WHEREAS, children, youth, and adults internalize and act on these cultural models, thereby tending to limit their sense of self-worth and dignity;

THEREFORE, BE IT RESOLVED: that the 1977 General Assembly of the Unitarian Universalist Association calls upon all Unitarian Universalists to examine carefully their own religious beliefs and the extent to which these beliefs influence sex-role stereotypes within their own families; and

BE IT FURTHER RESOLVED: that the General Assembly urges the Board of Trustees of the Unitarian Universalist Association to encourage the Unitarian Universalist Association to encourage the Unitarian Association administrative officers and staff, the religious leaders within societies, the Unitarian Universalist theological schools, the directors of related organizations, and the planners of seminars and conferences, to make every effort to: (a) put traditional assumptions and language in perspective, and (b) avoid sexist assumptions and language in the future.

BE IT FURTHER RESOLVED: that the General Assembly urges the President of the Unitarian Universalist Association to send copies of this resolution to other denominations examining sexism inherent in religious literature and institutions and to the International Association of Liberal Religious Women and the IARF (International Association for Religious Freedom); and

BE IT FURTHER RESOLVED: that the General Assembly requests the Unitarian Universalist Association (a) to join with those who are encouraging others in the society to examine the relationship between religious and cultural attitudes toward women, and (b) to send a representative and resource materials to associations appropriate to furthering the above goals; and

BE IT FURTHER RESOLVED: that the General Assembly requests the President of the UUA to report annually on progress in implementing this resolution.

1981 Proposed Bylaw Amendment

In the following proposed Bylaw Amendments, underlining indicates an insertion, brackets around the words indicate a deletion.

1.		The Association, dedicated to
2.		the principles of a free faith,
3.		shall:
4.	(a)	Support the free and disciplined
5.		search for truth as the [founda-
6.		tion of religious fellowship] <u>cen-</u>
7.		<u>ter of our religious community</u>;
8.	(b)	[Cherish and spread the univer-
9.		sal truths taught by the great
10.		prophets and teachers of human-
11.		ity in every age and tradition,
12.		immemorially summarized in
13.		the Judeo-Christian heritage as
14.		love of God and love of human-
15.		kind;] <u>Recognize our Judeo-</u>
16.		<u>Christian heritage as well as</u>
17.		<u>other traditions and seek last-</u>
18.		<u>ing values and new insights;</u>
19.	(c)	<u>Recognize the importance of</u>
20.		<u>equality among women and men;</u>

21. (c) (d)   Affirm, defend, and promote the
22.   supreme worth and dignity of
23.   every [human personality,] per-
24.   son;
25. (c) (c)   [And the use of] Support the
26.   democratic [method] process
27.   and mutual respect in all human
28.   relationships;
29. (d) (g)   [Implement the vision of one
30.   world by striving] Strive for a
31.   world community [founded on
32.   ideals of brotherhood] of love,
33.   justice and peace;
34. (e) (h)   Serve the needs of member
35.   societies.
36. (f) (i)   Organize new churches and fel-
37.   lowships and [otherwise] extend
38.   and strengthen liberal religion;
39. (g)   [Encourage cooperation among
40.   people of good will in every land.]

New Draft Amendment

(OFFERED BY THE BYLAWS REVISION COMMITTEE AT THE 1983 GENERAL ASSEMBLY OF THE UUA)

The Unitarian Universalist Association is empowered to and shall devote its resources to and exercise its corporate powers for religious, educational, and charitable purposes.

1. The purpose of the Association is to serve the needs of its member societies in the range and depth of their diversity, organize new societies, and otherwise extend and strengthen liberal religion.

Section C-2.2. Principles
1. In Unitarian Universalist
2. congregations people of diverse
3. religious viewpoints gather for
4. worship and celebration, study and
5. dialogue, companionship and
6. service.
7. The Unitarian Universalist Asso-
8. ciation is a voluntary association
9. of societies that value their distinct
10. origins and current religious life.

11. These societies reflect various
12. forms
13. of theism, Christianity, Human-
14. ism, Feminism, and other
15. religious
16. traditions. The Association shall
17. cherish, protect, and foster this
18. religious pluralism as a desirable
19. and enriching consequence of
20. religious freedom.
21. Within their diversity Unitarian
22. Universalist societies affirm their
23. dedication to the folllowing prin-
24. ciples and charge the Association to
25. defend and promote:
26. (a) a free and disciplined search for truth,
27. (b) love, mutual acceptance, and
28. personal growth in our religious
29. communities,
30. (c) the worth and dignity of every
31. person,
32. (d) equality and justice in human
33. relationships,
34. (e) the use of democratic processes
35. in the life of our societies and
36. the wider community,
37. (f) world community of love, justice,
38. and peace,
39. (g) the integrity of the earth and our
40. responsibility to protect its re-
41. sources for future generations.

Further Reading

Cassara, Ernest, Ed., *Universalism in America: A Documentary History of a Liberal Faith*, revised edition (Boston: Skinner House Books, 1997).

Gray, Elizabeth Dodson, Ed., *Sacred Dimensions of Women's Experience* (New York: Roundtable Press, 1988).

Howe, Charles, *For Faith and Freedom: A Short History of Unitarianism in Europe* (Boston: Skinner House Books, 1997).

Marshall, George N., *Challenge of a Liberal Faith* (Boston: Skinner House Books, 1988).

Parke, David B., *The Epic of Unitarianism* (Boston, Skinner House Books, 1985).

Robinson, Elmo, *American Universalism, Its Origins, Organization, and Heritage* (Boston: Beacon Press, 1971).

Sanger, Margaret, *An Autobiography* (New York: W.W. Norton & Co., 1938; Maxwell Reprint Co., 1970).

Schwartz, Tony, *What Really Matters, Searching for Wisdom in America* (New York: Bantam, 1995).

Wilbur, Earl M., *Our Unitarian Heritage: An Introduction to the History of the Unitarian Movement* (Boston: Beacon Press, 1963).

Williams, George Huntston, *American Universalism* (Boston: Skinner House Books, 1983).